D1605974

How Brands Grow
Part 2

This book is dedicated to Gerald Goodhardt, developer of the Dirichlet model and the duplication of viewing law—Gerald, you have taught us so much: your wisdom and wit have been much appreciated.

how brands grow

Part 2

*including emerging markets, services and
durables, new brands and luxury brands*

Jenni Romaniuk
Byron Sharp

OXFORD
UNIVERSITY PRESS
AUSTRALIA & NEW ZEALAND

OXFORD
UNIVERSITY PRESS

Oxford University Press is a department of the University of Oxford.
It furthers the University's objective of excellence in research,
scholarship, and education by publishing worldwide. Oxford is a registered
trademark of Oxford University Press in the UK and in certain other
countries.

Published in Australia by
Oxford University Press
253 Normanby Road, South Melbourne, Victoria 3205, Australia

National Library of Australia Cataloguing-in-Publication entry
    Creator: Romaniuk, Jenni, author.

    Title: How brands grow. Part 2, Including emerging markets, services and durables, new brands
        and luxury brands / Jenni Romaniuk, Byron Sharp.

    ISBN: 9780195596267 (hardback)

    Notes: Includes bibliographical references.

    Subjects: Marketing.
            Branding (Marketing)
            Brand name products—Management.
    Other Creators/Contributors: Sharp, Byron, author.

    Dewey Number: 658.827

Edited by Susan Keogh
Typeset by diacriTech, Chennai, India
Proofread by Pete Cruttenden
Printed by Sheck Wah Tong Printing Press Ltd.

Contents

Introduction

'My market is different.' It's a common refrain, and not untrue—every market has its peculiarities that have to be experienced and learnt on the job. This said, there are fundamental similarities about the ways brands compete and buyers buy, and hence how marketing works—otherwise marketers would find it near impossible to work effectively across different markets.

How Brands Grow Part 2 is about the fundamentals of buying behaviour and brand performance: fundamentals that provide a consistent roadmap for brand growth, and improved marketing productivity. Anyone who calls himself or herself a marketing professional should be aware of these fundamentals, but we wrote *How Brands Grow Part 2* with two particular audiences in mind.

First, this book is for readers of the first *How Brands Grow* who want to learn more about some of the key concepts and their application. For you, we have expanded on areas such as mental availability, physical availability, and how to leverage distinctive assets. Along the way we explain these concepts:

- why double jeopardy occurs, and the conditions where it does not
- how to analyse brand associations to manage and build mental availability
- the myth of Road to Damascus–style customer acquisition
- metrics to assess the strength of your distinctive brand assets.

Second, *How Brands Grow Part 2* is for marketers operating in areas such as emerging markets, services, e-commerce and luxury markets. We cover these categories, including examples from financial services, telecommunications, fast food, supermarket and fashion retailers, phone handsets and cars across a diverse set of countries from China and Brazil to Turkey and Nigeria.

We hope you enjoy *How Brands Grow Part 2*. Please do send us your feedback.

Jenni and Byron

Acknowledgments

We would like to thank the following people who reviewed early manuscripts pointing out errors and confusing writing: Zac Anesbury, Abou Bakar, Vivien Chanana, Francesca Dall'Olmo Riley, Margaret Faulkner, Kesten Green, Nicole Hartnett, Richard Lee, Larry Lockshin, Cathy Nguyen, Sarah Patrick, Anne Sharp, Lucy Simmonds, Arry Tanusondjaja, Quin Tran, Kelly Vaughan and Amy Wilson. We would also like to thank Sarah Patrick and Emily Primavera whose research assistance helped bring the data to the page. Thank you also to our colleagues at the Ehrenberg–Bass Institute for their general support and encouragement throughout the process of putting *How Brands Grow Part 2* together. Thank you as well to the Institute's corporate sponsors who provide feedback, data and constantly ask the difficult questions—in particular the members of our advisory boards in Europe, the USA and Australasia.

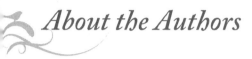

About the Authors

Jenni Romaniuk

Jenni Romaniuk is Research Professor and Associate Director (International) of the Ehrenberg–Bass Institute at the University of South Australia. Jenni's research covers brand equity, mental availability, brand health metrics, advertising effectiveness, distinctive assets, word of mouth and the role of loyalty in growth. She is the developer of the Distinctive Asset Grid, which is used by companies around the world to assess the strength and strategic potential of their brand's distinctive assets. She is also a pioneer in mental availability measurement and metrics.

Jenni is executive editor (international) of the *Journal of Advertising Research*, and is on the editorial review boards of four other journals. <www.JenniRomaniuk.com>

Byron Sharp

Dr Byron Sharp is Professor of Marketing Science and the Director of the Ehrenberg–Bass Institute at the University of South Australia.

Byron's book *How Brands Grow* was voted marketing book of the year by AdAge readers in 2013. He has published over 100 academic papers and is on the editorial board of five journals. He recently co-hosted, with Professor Jerry Wind, two conferences at the Wharton Business School on the laws of advertising, and co-edited the 2009 and 2013 special issues of the *Journal of Advertising Research* on scientific laws of advertising.

His university textbook *Marketing: Theory, Evidence, Practice* (Oxford University Press) was released in 2013.
<www.ByronSharp.com>

Magda Nenycz-Thiel

Dr Magda Nenycz-Thiel is a Senior Researcher at the Ehrenberg–Bass Institute at the University of South Australia. Magda's main research area is retailing, with particular focus on private-label brands, category growth and online shopping behaviour. She has published in international journals such as the *Journal of Business Research*, *Journal of Advertising Research* and *Journal of Marketing Management*. She is associate editor of the *Journal of Consumer Behaviour*.

Robert East

Robert East is Emeritus Professor of Consumer Behaviour at Kingston Business School, London, and Adjunct Professor at Ehrenberg–Bass Institute at the University of South Australia. He trained as a social psychologist and is a postgraduate of London Business School. His research focuses on store use, consumer loyalty and brand switching and word-of-mouth patterns. Robert East is the founding author of an evidence-based textbook, *Consumer Behaviour: Applications in Marketing* (2013) published by Sage.

About the Ehrenberg–Bass Institute

The Ehrenberg–Bass Institute at the University of South Australia Business School is a university based R&D thinktank devoted to advancing marketing science. Its research is used and financially supported by many of the world's leading corporations, including Coca-Cola, Colgate-Palmolive, First National Bank, General Motors, Procter & Gamble, Turner Broadcasting, CBS, ESPN, and Unilever. For more on the Institute go to www.marketingscience.info

1

How Brands Grow

Byron Sharp and Jenni Romaniuk

This chapter quickly ends the debate about whether sales growth comes from *penetration* (getting more customers) or *loyalty* (getting customers to buy more). It documents the law of double jeopardy, with examples from a number of areas:

- emerging markets
- industrial (business-to-business, or B2B)
- services
- durables
- across local and global brands
- a wide range of loyalty metrics.

We explain *why* double jeopardy occurs, and describe the conditions under which brands do, and do not, conform to the double jeopardy law.

How to grow

'Grow to survive' is a marketing mantra. Even in high-growth markets, growing market share is necessary to gain scale, to match the marketing budgets of rivals, and to have a positive momentum story to explain to retailers why your product should be on shelves in the face of competition.

It's easy for managers of small brands to waste time on inconsequential efforts or even damage the brand by unnecessary change. Likewise it is easy for managers of large brands to be lulled into complacency by consistently high metrics and allow a more nimble competitor to erode share. Throughout *How Brands Grow Part 2*, we highlight the important strategies marketers can use, but also the pitfalls that marketers can face.

In this chapter we'll show how much penetration matters for growth and how loyalty metrics can be predicted from a brand's penetration.

Can you engineer your brand loyalty?

A fundamental question of marketing strategy is whether to focus on improving the loyalty of existing customers or to try to win new customers. Logic says that both are ways to grow but logic alone often fails to tell us how the real world works. Are both equally attractive options for growth?

The loyalty path delivers extra sales revenue through existing customers buying more (and therefore less of competitors' brands). Such a strategy might focus on improving the attractiveness of the brand to these customers: for example, through better service, rewarding loyalty with incentives or points, or offering existing customers related products or services (cross-selling).

Loyalty strategies are thought to lower marketing costs through having a much narrower advertising target, as existing customers are just a fraction of the market. Further, it is thought that, given these customers already buy the brand, they do not need as much encouragement or inducement to buy compared to non-buyers. This makes these additional sales cheaper, and if these buyers are cheaper to reach and cheaper to convert, the loyalty strategy generates a higher return on investment (ROI).

A similar strategy is to focus on customer retention, which offers the promise of increasing the size of the customer base though reducing customer defections. While not focusing on acquisition might sound like an odd way to grow a customer base, it is often claimed that a loyalty strategy will, as a by-product, create brand advocates who generate positive word of mouth that attracts new customers and, at least, maintains acquisition levels. Coupled with greater retention, this strategy should, hypothetically, grow the customer base. This rationale includes accepting the (mythical) claim that focusing on retention rather than acquisition is a cheaper way to maintain a customer base.

It turns out that all this speculation is for naught, and *How Brands Grow* (2010) presented decades of evidence that renders this question largely moot: brands grow by improving both penetration and loyalty, though typically far more sales growth comes from gains in penetration than improved loyalty. The question of whether strategy should therefore aim for loyalty or penetration has a very clear answer. Brands can enjoy higher loyalty, *but only if they very substantially improve their penetration*. A loyalty-first approach is simply not a growth strategy. Given how overwhelming the evidence is, it is very surprising that many marketing consultants and academics still propose the sort of logic (and hopes) presented in the previous paragraphs.

Having one clear path to growth need not stifle creativity in marketing. Engineers build aeroplanes in different ways but all methods draw on the same scientific evidence as to which materials to use, and all aeroplane designers must work with the laws of motion and gravity. Similarly, marketing choices—about what media to advertise in, who to target, the creative direction of a campaign, the price point, and even the product formulation—need to work with the law-like patterns of competitive markets. All of these choices, if successful, will result in the same underlying pattern of growth. As a brand grows, it gains a predictable amount of penetration and loyalty for its market share. This real-world pattern is known as *the law of double jeopardy*.

The law of double jeopardy

Double jeopardy was identified in the 1960s by a sociologist, William McPhee (McPhee, 1963). He noticed this phenomenon in attitudinal data: for example, less well-known radio announcers (the first jeopardy) are also less liked by those who know them (the second jeopardy).

A decade later Andrew Ehrenberg (1972) and Claude Martin (1973) independently documented this same pattern in brand choice: smaller share brands have fewer sales because they have many fewer customers (the first jeopardy) who are slightly less loyal (the second jeopardy).

Since then the law of double jeopardy has been observed for industrial brands, services, stores, store chains, comic strips, newspapers, radio stations, television networks, television programs and politicians. In Table 1.1 are two examples from industrial (B2B) settings: concrete suppliers and coronary stents (components used by hospitals in surgical procedures).

Table 1.1: Double jeopardy in industrial markets

	Concrete suppliers		Coronary stents	
	Penetration (%)	Purchase frequency (3-month average)	Penetration (%)	Purchase frequency (6-month average)
A	46	2.96	18	8.4
B	36	1.54	15	3.2
C	35	1.46	12	3.2
D	31	1.27	8	5.2*
E	26	1.03	8	3.0

*The obvious deviation is due to a single buyer making many purchases in a short time period. These exceptions happen, though they rarely persist.

Sources: Pickford & Goodhardt, 2000 (concrete suppliers); McCabe, Stern & Dacko, 2013 (coronary stents)

When brands are listed in market share order we can easily see that both penetration and loyalty metrics decline in line with lower market share. This holds for local and global brands: see Table 1.2, where Colgate in China has about double the market share of LSL (a local brand).

Table 1.2: Illustration of the double jeopardy law—toothpaste in China (annual figures for 2011)

Brands	Market share (%)	Household penetration (%)	Average purchase frequency (number of times purchased)	Average share of category purchases (%)
Crest	19	57	2.8	29
Colgate	14	46	2.5	26
Zhonghua	12	43	2.4	25
Darlie	11	35	2.7	26
LSL	6	23	2.2	23
Hei mei	3	14	1.9	18
YNBY	3	14	2.2	20
Bamboo	2	9	2.0	19
LMZ	2	9	1.7	17
Sensodyne	0.3	2	1.5	13
Average	**7**	**25**	**2.2**	**22**

Source: Kantar Worldpanel China

It also has double the penetration (46 versus 23%), and a bit higher loyalty (purchase frequency of 2.5 compared with 2.2, and share of category buying of 26% compared with 23%).

Two brands with similar market share will typically have these two characteristics:

- very similar penetration levels—that is, the number of people who buy them, at least once, during the time period of interest
- highly similar levels of loyalty—that is, the people who buy them will, on average, buy them at similar rates, devote similar proportions of their repertoire, repeat-buy at the same rate, and so on.

A brand could, theoretically, enjoy similar sales to a rival brand but have a much smaller but more loyal customer base—the classic niche brand—*but this hardly ever happens*. Small market-share brands practically always have the penetration and the loyalty metrics expected of small brands, and even small brands that are slightly niche still rarely have the loyalty levels of large brands.

Table 1.2 also counters the myth that Chinese consumers aren't loyal to brands and always shop on price (for example, The Economist, 2014). One of the pioneers in buyer behaviour research in China, Professor Mark Uncles, set up a panel of buyers in China over a decade ago to observe their retail and brand buying behaviour. His team was among the very first to report double jeopardy in China, with smaller retailers and brands having systematically lower penetration and loyalty than larger share brands (Uncles, 2010; Uncles & Kwok, 2008). From the durable sector, Bennett (2008) reported double jeopardy for buying televisions in China.

Chinese customers are loyal to brands, just not 100% loyal (few people are). Armed with the knowledge of double jeopardy, you can see the brand loyalty patterns for Chinese consumers for what they are—largely normal, with occasional typical exceptions.

Figure 1.1: Double jeopardy chart for soft drinks in (a) Nigeria and (b) Kenya (2014)

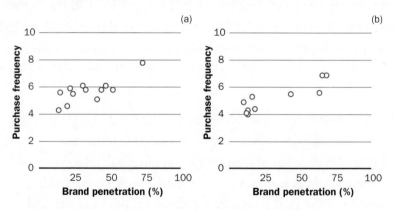

Double jeopardy occurs for packaged goods, services, durables—a wide range of categories and in every country where it has been tested. In Figure 1.1, we show examples from Nigeria and Kenya in soft drinks and, in Table 1.3, we see the double jeopardy pattern in Indonesian banking—across different loyalty metrics such as number of products bought, attitudes and defection rates (with the pattern in reverse, where big brands have smaller defection rates).

Larger share brands have many more customers, who buy them a little more often than smaller share brands.

Table 1.3: Double jeopardy across metrics for personal banking in Indonesia (2014)

Brands	Penetration (%)	Average number of products per customer	Customers who say brand is their favourite (%)	Potential defection p.a. (%)
Bank Central Asia	64	1.8	57	13
Bank Mandiri	63	1.9	48	17
Bank Rakyat Indonesia	50	1.6	41	17
Bank Negara Indonesia	49	1.7	43	17
Bank Tabungan Negara	20	1.5	19	36
Average	**49**	**1.7**	**42**	**20**

When brands grow or decline, their movements do not depart from the double jeopardy pattern. Gains (or losses) in market share conform to double jeopardy—so as brands gain (or lose) penetration their loyalty metrics also simultaneously adjust. This means that looking at a single annual or quarterly snapshot of brand performance metrics won't reveal which brand is growing or declining. Researchers have looked at deviations from double jeopardy to see if this might foretell a brand's movement and have found that it doesn't (Kearns, Millar & Lewis, 2000). Brands do not, as commonly asserted, kick off growth with unusually high loyalty for their current size. Nor do we see brands develop unusually low loyalty (for their penetration) before they decline. Another marketing myth dies.

In other words, growing and declining brands look normal for their current market share. This means that in any category, two 10% share brands will each have similar penetrations and very similar loyalty metrics—even if one brand was 11% last year and is headed downwards, and the other was 9% last year and is heading upwards. Currently they are both 10% brands so their metrics look like a 10% brand should. And when they move to a new level of market share, they look normal for that new level. This is another nail in the coffin for loyalty-focused growth strategies. If they did work, we would surely by now have evidence of a brand having excess loyalty that it parlayed into market-share growth.

What we have is clear evidence that the growth and decline in the size of a brand's customer base (penetration) is due largely to unusual acquisition levels. Both growing and declining brands lose customers essentially in line with expected defection rates (as dictated by their respective market shares). It's the level of acquisition that largely determines if brands grow or decline. If acquisition is higher than expected, the brand will grow; if it is lower than expected, the brand will decline (Riebe et al., 2014). Detroit's loss of US market share to Japanese and then Korean brands was not due to collapsing retention rates, but rather because US car brands failed to win their usual share of customer acquisition (Sharp, 2009). It's as if you can only control one lever to grow penetration, and that is your acquisition rate.

We see double jeopardy in every category we explore, such as banking, insurance, retailers, social media sites, mobile phones, and B2B, and in every country from China to Russia, from Nigeria to South Africa, from Turkey to Indonesia. Indeed, testing has only been limited by data availability. But don't just take our word for it: look in your own data—all you need to do is organise the brands by market share.

Penetration rules!

Most changes in market share will show up as larger movements in penetration and smaller increases in loyalty metrics. This is the way double jeopardy says it has to be because most brands are a long way from owning most of the market (that is, more than 70% market share) and so have modest levels of penetration even if the metric is calculated for a whole year[1]. It's been shown many times that most brands sit on the low to middle part of the double jeopardy line (Allsopp, Sharp & Dawes, 2004; Ehrenberg, Goodhardt & Barwise, 1990; Uncles et al., 1994). A move from one position to another on the double jeopardy line then typically means large changes in penetration accompanied by small changes in loyalty.

Supporting this are studies of small market-share changes (such as from one year to the next) that have shown growth and decline reveal changes much more in penetration than brand loyalty (Anschuetz, 2002; Baldinger, Blair & Echambadi, 2002; McDonald & Ehrenberg, 2003; Romaniuk, Dawes & Nenycz-Thiel, 2014a, b; Sylvester, McQueen & Moore, 1994).

Table 1.4 shows a brand that doubled its share in Brazil over a four-year period. Penetration rose by 82%, explaining most of this increase in sales, while changes in loyalty metrics over this period were less dramatic (around 35%). It had many more customers buy it somewhat more often.

Table 1.4: An example of a brand growing over time—toothpaste in Brazil (2006–09)

Year	Market share (%)	Household penetration (%)	Average purchase frequency	Average share of category requirements
2006	6.3	22	2.3	16
2007	10.1	31	2.8	19
2008	11.7	35	2.9	20
2009	14.1	40	3.1	22
% change 2006–09	124	82	35	38

Source: Nielsen Household Panel Brazil

1   We now generally advise brand managers not to use annual penetration, but rather use quarterly (three-monthly) brand metrics. This gives a more realistic picture and fits with the frequency of new marketing interventions.

The exceptions to double jeopardy can occur when brands have extremely high penetration, or are genuinely trapped in a niche, with a very high penetration of a very limited market (for example, brands that have only been able to secure regional distribution). In these circumstances brands will see their growth (or decline) reflected mostly in loyalty metrics simply because of the ceiling on penetration.

A niche brand simply has restricted growth potential. This makes large marketing investments unwise unless these limitations can be dealt with (such as securing more distribution). Niche brands should be pitied for their lack of potential, rather than celebrated. Small brands are better than niche brands—they *can* become big.

Why does double jeopardy occur?

In competitive choice situations, where buyers have a range of not-too-dissimilar options to buy, brands still have large differences:

- *mental availability*—which is the propensity for the brand to be thought of in buying situations; and
- *physical availability*—which is how easy the brand is to buy and find.

We explore the underpinnings of mental and physical availability throughout *How Brands Grow Part 2*.

Large popular brands will have excellent mental and physical availability amongst the buying population. This means more people will buy them (higher penetration). Small brands will have far less mental and physical availability. Indeed some people don't even know these brands exist, and many potential buyers seldom, if ever, notice them. Therefore fewer people buy them (lower penetration) in any time period.

But why do brands also vary in their loyalty scores, and vary systematically in line with their size? Again the answer lies in mental and physical availability and the fact that these combine to be the dominant driver of a brand's market share. It means that very popular brands are thought of by more people across more category-buying occasions, and are available to buy in some places where they are the sole brand (or one of very few). Similarly many light or infrequent buyers of the category don't know of many brands, and the few brands these buyers do know are much more likely to be the larger brands.

Small brands unenviably find themselves in the opposite position. Fewer people know them and fewer know them well, while the people who do know them tend to be heavier category buyers—and these people also buy many other brands, including the big brands. Small brands are available in fewer outlets and these tend to be common locations (such as the largest supermarkets) where they are displayed alongside many other (larger) competitors.

The higher competition faced by small brands is illustrated in Figure 1.2 for fast food brands in Russia and South Korea. In both cases, a small brand's customers *buy many more other brands* than the customers of big brands do. For example in Russia, customers of the biggest brand, McDonald's, also buy from 2.6 other quick-service food brands; while in the same time period, customers of the much smaller Sbarro's buy from more than twice as many brands (5.6). This law-like pattern is known as the *natural monopoly law*, a title that refers to the fact that larger share brands have a greater proportion of their customer base made up of light category buyers (and therefore monopolise the light category buyers).

These differences mean that the customers of smaller brands know about and buy many more options. Even if you buy a small brand for the first time and really like it, its competitive conditions make it a bit harder to remember that brand (mental availability) and, even if you do, a bit harder to find it (physical availability). Likewise if, sitting in McDonald's, you decide that you really didn't like the burger you just ate, the odds are you'll still probably eat there again one day because it's just so easy—McDonald's is in your head, and it is widely physically available.

If the big difference (in terms of what drives choice) between the brands is their availability (mental and physical) then we have to have

Figure 1.2: Smaller share brands attract heavy category buyers for fast food in (a) Russia and (b) South Korea (2014)

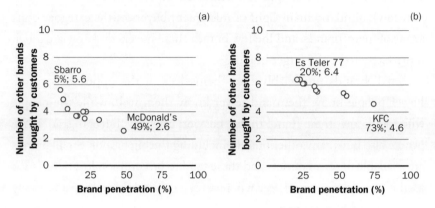

double jeopardy, where high penetration brands also enjoy slightly higher loyalty metrics.

If we refer back to our Indonesian banking example in Table 1.3 Bank Tabungan Negara (BTN) has a defection rate much higher than the other Indonesian banks listed. This is not because BTN's customers are particularly unhappy or its service is bad—but simply a function of two factors:

- a limited product range focusing on loans for subsidised housing, rather than the more traditional product mix aiming towards transaction account customers, which constrains mental availability; and
- fewer branches (only 100 branches), compared to Bank Mandiri (around 2000 branches) and Bank Rakyat Indonesia (around 4000 branches), which constrains physical availability.

Much of the defection in financial services is driven by customers changing their circumstances—they move, get married, have children—and smaller brands with fewer locations, fewer branches and less well-known product ranges are particularly vulnerable to these changes, so they get higher defection (lower loyalty).

A brand's loyalty levels relate to its penetration level; both are underpinned by mental and physical availability. This double jeopardy pattern wouldn't occur if a brand were really differentiated from others, such that it appealed to or 'locked in' a specific type of customer.

Store brands (for example, the brands of particular supermarket chains) are a commonly cited (mild) exception to double jeopardy. These brands have restricted penetration because they are stocked in only one chain. This means that store brand metrics often look like slight outliers to the double jeopardy pattern, with a niche pattern of lower penetration than expected and higher loyalty metrics (see also Dawes, 2013; Pare & Dawes, 2011)—though not if the metrics are calculated for sales within that store chain, within that chain's shoppers. Then store brands enjoy largely normal levels of loyalty for their share in that chain's sales.

Truong (2014) documented double jeopardy deviations across six emerging markets (Brazil, China, India, Indonesia, Malaysia and the Philippines). Across more than 450 brands in twenty repeat purchase categories, only 10% of brands deviated substantially from their expected loyalty level. *No* systematic exceptions existed in any of these categories:

- local brands
- global brands
- higher priced brands
- discount brands
- country of origin.

Half of the exceptions were dominant market leaders displaying a little 'excess loyalty', similar to that sometimes observed in developed markets (Fader & Schmittlein, 1993; Pare & Dawes, 2011). The remaining exceptions were split, with some having higher and others lower than expected loyalty, with no clear patterns or explanation.

Deviations from double jeopardy are therefore relatively unusual and, when they are present, they are not usually terribly dramatic or insightful. Deviating brands rarely command the sort of super loyalty that marketers dream of, unless the brand is already extremely dominant in penetration. In fact, for brands with unusual loyalty levels, the story usually isn't one of stellar loyalty at all, but rather that the deviation simply reflects restricted penetration. For example, the geography of many emerging markets means that local brands are often regionally based, and lack full distribution across the country; this restricts their total market penetration, so their loyalty level can look high for this (low) penetration, similar to store brands only distributed in a single retail chain. This is often mistaken for strong loyalty.

On rare occasions brands have low loyalty for their level of penetration; this tends to be because they are bought for a particular occasion, need, or time of year. This often reveals an issue with category definition. For example, premium whisky brands, which are typically purchased for special occasions (fiftieth birthdays) or given as gifts, when analysed alongside standard whisky brands, look different. But, when mixed with other premium whisky brands, these brands look normal.

Interestingly, the conditions that would make a category depart from double jeopardy—highly differentiated brands each appealing to particular segments—are widely assumed by marketing theorists to be normal or commonplace. Unfortunately many market research reports fuel this misconception by routinely reporting (tiny) differences in brand customer base demographics, and showing charts that (misleadingly) suggest large perceived differentiation. If this really were the case, we would not have a double jeopardy law—but we do. In the real world, double jeopardy is everywhere and exceptions are usually small. Differentiation turns out to be slight, and of far less consequence than thought (for further evidence, see *How Brands Grow*). In line with this, substantive deviations from double jeopardy are uncommon and tend to be easily explained.

Double jeopardy is clearly evident in most markets, for most brands. This is not a pattern exclusive to the stable, mature markets that dominate the developed world. It is also evident in dynamic emerging markets, services, durables and even B2B markets. Even in categories with obvious functional differences between brands, we tend to see surprisingly small exceptions to the law of double jeopardy.

For example, *1st for Women* insurance in South Africa claims to design insurance products especially for women, and indeed 90% of its customer base is female (compared to an average of around 50% for other brands). This is pretty atypical, yet its loyalty, expressed as the number of products held is 1.9, only a little higher than expected given its low penetration (see Table 1.5).

Table 1.5: Double jeopardy in insurance in South Africa (2012)

Brands	Penetration (%)	Insurance products held with company
Outsurance	27	2.3
Mutual & Federal	13	2.3
Santam	12	2.5
ABSA idirect	11	2.1
Auto & General	10	2.0
Budget	7	1.9
AA	7	1.3
Dial Direct	6	1.9
St Bank/Stanbic	5	2.0
Miway	4	1.8
1st for women	3	1.9
Average	**10**	**2.0**

Source: National Advertising Bureau Roots Survey 2012

How to grow

Double jeopardy provides a clear strategy lesson. It is not possible to grow market share without reaching category buyers who never or very seldom buy your brand. Focusing on your current consumers, particularly your heavier consumers, sounds efficient. It's human nature to prefer to talk to those who already know and like us. However, this strategy won't deliver much in the way of sales growth, and could indeed set you back as you lose the lighter customers you neglect, and fail to acquire new customers. We talk more about this in Chapter 2.

In emerging markets, a focus on current customers misses a great opportunity to capitalise on category expansion and attract these new category buyers to your brand. Winning a share of these new buyers is essential in order to enjoy the category growth. If a 10% share brand wants to stay a 10% share brand it must continuously win 10% of the new buyers entering the category.

The good news is that if you recruit them, *and* you have a product that is good enough to do the job it was bought to do, *and* you keep up mental and physical availability, then you will get repeat purchases. Loyalty will be a natural consequence of effective marketing that builds the customer base and grows penetration. The more effective your marketing is at building the customer base, the more loyalty you will receive.

Dismantling barriers to market-share growth

The first step towards an evidence-based growth strategy is to remove any self-inflicted barriers. The organic growth occurring in some categories or markets can blind you to faults in your own strategy: sales are rising, revenue is looking good, but competitors may in effect be pushing you out of the market by reaching places or buyers you are ignoring. A growth-oriented strategy has to be a market penetration-oriented strategy. And tactics aimed at reaching out to new customers usually can't help to also reach existing customers, who have a heightened tendency to notice the brand's marketing activities (Harrison, 2013). Reaching out to non-customers and light customers does not neglect your current customer base, but strategies only aimed at your brand's existing customer base can easily exclude non-buyers.

Beware of consultants selling you loyalty initiatives that promise to deliver growth by targeting your existing customers, or worse, your heaviest existing customers. One fad that was popular in developed economies was to sell loyalty programs and customer relationship management (CRM) software and staff training on the basis that it would stem defection and result in existing customers buying many more services. But both before and after this all started, cross-selling metrics obeyed the double jeopardy law.

For example, in spite of all their efforts, banks vary only a little in terms of how many products their customers have with them—and this in line with their size, whether or not they have adopted a particular CRM system or whatever their customer satisfaction scores were. The bigger banks with much higher penetration have slightly higher cross-product loyalty, as double jeopardy says should be the case (see Figure 1.3, which shows metrics for banks in India).

Figure 1.3: Double jeopardy in banks in India (2014)

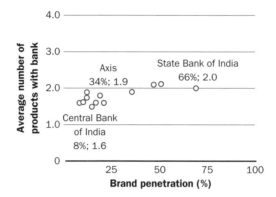

In South Africa, we discovered that one of our sponsors, First National Bank, had been told that they needed to target their existing customers with cross-selling initiatives. It wasn't working. They had been told that Wells Fargo in the USA had achieved outstanding cross-product loyalty, well ahead of its peers. We doubted this immediately (financial analysts shared our doubts according to *The Wall Street Journal* (Smith, 2011)).

Figure 1.3 clearly shows that banks with much higher penetration only have slightly more cross-product loyalty from its customers. If Central Bank of India achieved a miracle and its customers had on average four products (double the market leader) it would still be one of the smaller banks in India. The State Bank of India would still be vastly larger because it has almost ten times the number of customers.

First National Bank of South Africa's management listened to us and made a decisive and well-implemented strategic turnaround to a penetration strategy. They are now the second-largest and fastest-growing bank in South Africa. Over the past five years, a very difficult time for banks, FNB has grown its customer base from 5.8 to 7.5 million (a rise of 29%); meanwhile the number of products per customer has increased from just 2.03 to 2.1 (a rise of 3%) in line with double jeopardy. FNB is the market leader in mobile banking with a 33% share of the market despite its 23% share of all banking and it has added 1.3 million customers to its online banking offer, a rise of 27% in the twelve months ending September 2012. FNB was also voted the most innovative bank in the world (Finance Global Banking Awards, Washington DC, 2012), while Bernice Samuels, the chief marketing officer, was recognised as Marketing Personality of the Year. (See Bayne, Samuels & Sharp, 2014 for the full story.)

The conclusion is clear. The first place to look for growth barriers is your own marketing strategy—it may be holding you back. Another place to look for penetration barriers are impediments to purchase. Is anything making it difficult to buy or use your brand? Do you have varieties to suit most buyers? Are you too expensive for the mainstream customer?

In the USA people live in houses and drive cars that are very large by emerging market standards. This allows them to buy large packages and in quantities that are impractical in other countries (where in the house could they be stored?)—these are barriers to penetration in some countries. In Thailand, a great market for haircare products, premium Western brands are desirable, but large bottles were beyond the weekly budget of many households. Companies like L'Oréal, Unilever and Procter & Gamble found success in offering much smaller packages of their brands. This might seem slightly counter-intuitive from a developed market perspective, as smaller packages mean that the product is more expensive per gram. Why would you market a more expensive product to people who weren't wealthy? But the smaller product lowers the overall price of purchase, the *entry cost*, which was a key barrier to penetration. Now millions could buy it, as an occasional treat, and it could be bought more regularly by hair-conscious teenagers, who were never going to save up for a large pricey bottle.

Our colleague Johan Bruwer has studied barriers to wine consumption in both developed and emerging markets. The biggest barrier in all markets is the perceived complexity in purchasing and consuming wine, compared to other alcoholic beverages. If buyers don't know brands or grape varieties this makes purchase difficult, even intimidating. The need for (and potential return from) wine education, for retailers and consumers, is obvious (Ovington et al., 2014), though not to all wine marketers. In India, amongst the population who drink alcohol, wine is perceived as a beverage for particular consumption situations—social and celebratory situations—and this limits purchase opportunities. For wine consumption to rise, consumers need to see people drinking wine in other situations, ideally more everyday situations.

Someone once predicted that wine would not move beyond its perception as drink for a 'special occasions' in the USA until wine was made in all fifty states. Today that is true (though it did take almost 300 years of wine production), and the USA is now the world's largest market for wine.

Interestingly the similarities of potential wine drinkers in a country like India far outweigh the differences with potential wine drinkers in Australia, the USA and the UK. The only clear difference is Indian consumers' fear of encountering fake wine, currently a real problem in this market (as in other alcohol categories such as whisky), and a barrier to penetration.

Meaningful loyalty metrics

Knowing about double jeopardy has the added practical value of giving loyalty metrics context and meaning. For example, it reveals if you have a niche or change-of-pace brand: both are deviations you may need to try to fix. If these deviations can't be fixed, then investment can be structured to reflect the brand's limited potential for growth.

Conclusion

The law of double jeopardy holds in emerging and developed markets, for services and products, in consumer and industrial categories. It has held for decades and continues to do so even as the markets globalise, and digital and mobile offerings change how we engage with and buy brands. Even in categories such as financial services, with state ownership of banks and much regulation, we see double jeopardy.

Consequently, for a brand to grow it needs to grow its market penetration, through broadening mental and physical availability. Targeted strategies to build loyalty without simultaneously having a much larger effect on the brand's penetration are unlikely to succeed. Focusing too much on loyalty, either by trying to build it or imagining it doesn't exist and thinking that you therefore need to 'buy' customers every time with price promotions or loyalty incentives, are costly distractions that brands can ill afford.

Double jeopardy exists because consumers are naturally loyal and because they are choosing between competitive (similar) offerings that vary a great deal in mental and physical availability from person to person and across the whole market.

Don't assume that any special characteristics about a brand will confer on it a loyalty advantage. If the brand does deviate from double jeopardy, search for impediments to penetration (such as lack of distribution in key regions or channels) as these may be what makes the loyalty metrics look high. And these impediments will limit growth potential.

The double jeopardy law tells us that brand growth depends on reaching non-customers and light customers. In Chapter 2, we'll look at these buyers. We'll discuss their strategic importance and the marketing challenges of reaching and refreshing the mental structures of many low-value customers.

FURTHER READING ON THE DOUBLE JEOPARDY LAW

Important claims require serious evidence, hence the many data sets in this chapter. Those interested in delving deeper or simply seeing the wide range of conditions under which the double jeopardy law has been documented (for example, attitudes, behaviour, industrial, services, durables, retail stores, voting, media) may wish to read the following peer-reviewed journal articles.

Bennett, Dag & Graham, Charles 2010, 'Is loyalty driving growth for the brand in front? A two-purchase analysis of car category dynamics in Thailand', *Journal of Strategic Marketing*, vol. 18, no. 7, pp. 573–85.

Bhat, S & Fox, R 1996, 'An investigation of jeopardy effects in store choice', *Journal of Retailing and Consumer Services*, vol 3, no. 3, pp. 129–33.

Donthu, N 1994, 'Double jeopardy in television program choice', *Journal of the Academy of Marketing Science*, vol. 22, no. 2, pp. 180–5.

Ehrenberg, Andrew 1972, *Repeat Buying: Theory and Applications*, American Elsevier, New York.

Ehrenberg, Andrew 1991, 'Politicians' double jeopardy: a pattern and exceptions', *Journal of the Market Research Society*, vol. 33, no. 1, pp. 347–53.

Ehrenberg, Andrew & Goodhardt, Gerald 2002, 'Double jeopardy revisited, again', Marketing Insights, *Marketing Research*, Spring, pp. 40–2.

Ehrenberg, Andrew, Goodhardt, Gerald & Barwise, Patrick 1990, 'Double jeopardy revisited', *Journal of Marketing*, vol. 54 (July), pp. 82–91.

McDowell, WS & Dick, SJ 2001, 'Using TV daypart double jeopardy effects to boost advertising efficiency', *Journal of Advertising Research*, vol. 41, no. 6, pp. 43–51.

McDowell, WS & Dick, SJ 2005, 'Revealing a double jeopardy effect in radio station audience behavior', *Journal of Media Economics*, vol. 18, no. 4, pp. 271–84.

Martin, C., Jr 1973 'The theory of double jeopardy', *Journal of the Academy of Marketing Science*, vol. 1, no. 2, pp. 148–56.

Michael, JH & Smith, PM 1999, 'The theory of double jeopardy: an example from a forest products industry', *Forest Products Journal*, vol. 49, no. 3, pp. 21–6.

Sharp, Byron & Riebe, Erica 2005, 'Does triple jeopardy exist for retail chains?', *Journal of Empirical Generalisations in Marketing Science*, vol. 9, <www.empgens.com/ArticlesHome/Articles.html>, viewed 7 July 2015.

Solgaard, H, Smith, D & Schmidt, M 1998, 'Double jeopardy patterns for political parties', *International Journal of Public Opinion Research*, vol. 10, no. 2, pp. 109–20.

Uncles, Mark & Lee, D 2006, 'Brand purchasing by older consumers: an investigation using the Juster scale and the Dirichlet model', *Marketing Letters*, vol. 17, no. 1, pp. 17–29.

Wright, Malcolm, Sharp, Anne & Sharp, Byron 1998, 'Are Australasian brands different?', *Journal of Brand and Product Management*, vol. 7, no. 6, pp. 465–80.
(A full reference list is at the end of this book.)

2

Target the (Whole) Market

Byron Sharp and Jenni Romaniuk

In Chapter 1, we talked about the double jeopardy law, which says that for a brand to grow, it needs to increase its penetration: that is, to win more customers in each time period. In this chapter we explore the nature of brand customer bases in more detail. We show why reaching very light and non-buyers of the brand, and light buyers of the category, are essential for growth. Along the way we further expose the heavy-buyer fallacy.

The scientific laws revealed in this chapter have major implications for brand strategy—from brand equity to media planning, to what to put in advertising. These laws explain why successful marketers are sophisticated mass marketers who have a deep and evolving understanding of *both* the commonalities *and* differences in their buyers, and use this understanding to appeal to a wide range of category buyers.

All that glitters ...

When the market is large, and full of unknowns, it is tempting to retreat from battling the whole market and focus on protecting what you have: your current customers, and particularly the ones that buy the brand often. Similarly, return on investment (ROI)–driven thinking encourages a focus on heavy or current customers. In this chapter we provide evidence to help prevent falling for loyalty myths.

We'll start by explaining why heavy customers are a poor source of *growth*.

The heavy buyer fallacy

Heavy buyers look attractive from a marketing perspective. They are worth more, much more, than the typical buyer of the brand. But, and this is very important, this isn't what matters from a growth perspective. What matters for growth is how much more they can be encouraged to buy from you. The answer turns out to be not much.

The first, and rather obvious reason, is that these people are few. A typical brand that might have, say, an average purchase frequency of only three times annually, and the top 20% might buy it at a rate of around five or six times annually. If all these heavy buyers made one more purchase in a year, which is a lot for that group (an increase of around 20%), this will actually deliver only a few per cent of sales growth because they are few in number. Simple maths.

Which brings us to the second, less obvious, reason. Contrary to popular belief, it isn't easy to boost the purchasing of your heaviest buyers. A brand's heaviest customers are already highly likely to be heavy buyers of the category, so it is unlikely that they will increase their category buying rate and buy even more, and you can't steal from competitors as they are already very loyal to the brand (Sharp, Trinh & Dawes, 2014). So where would the extra sales come from?

A brand's existing favouritism with heavy buyers puts a ceiling on how many more sales you can ever hope to gain from them. Heavy buyers aren't new to the category; this isn't something they are getting into; they are mature buyers of the category (think of them like a mature, saturated sub-market); and they already favour your brand. If a brand grows, we find surprisingly little of this is due to a brand's heaviest buyers.

Of course we want to retain these people as buyers of our brand. We want to reach them with your marketing efforts—and we almost always do. These buyers are vastly more likely to notice any marketing we do: they see our discounts; they notice our service improvements. Their brains are also far more attuned to noticing and recognising our brand, and its advertising. We hardly have to worry about giving these people extra attention: we are already in their sight line.

It would be nice to think that by focusing on these heavier buyers we could somehow reduce their defection risk but, in the original *How Brands Grow*, we saw that most customer defection is for reasons completely outside our control—for reasons such as customers moving house, getting married or dying. For example, in an Ehrenberg–Bass Institute study of business clients who had defected from their financial services provider, about 60% of defection occurred for reasons completely beyond the influence of marketers (Bogomolova & Romaniuk, 2009). For the remaining 40%, the key reasons were getting a cheaper offer from a competitor or joining some corporate buying group to gain cheaper services. Only 4% of business owners changed financial service provider because of a service issue—not exactly an incentive to introduce costly service improvement initiatives!

It would be nice to think that we could cross-sell other services to our customers to grow, but again the empirical evidence suggests this is very difficult as service brands vary little in the number of products their customers hold (Mundt, Dawes & Sharp, 2006). Besides, these people are a small part of your customer base, and a tiny part of your total potential market.

These strategies directed at heavy buyers are hit and miss at best and, even if you hit, the rewards are small.

Finally, it would be nice to think our heavy buyers become advocates and help us grow by recommending the brand—but the reality is that most word of mouth comes from lighter buyers, because these people are many. For example, we surveyed customers of Matahari, a popular department store chain in Indonesia, and found that the 11% of its heavier shoppers, who visit it three or times a month, accounted for only 15% of the word of mouth given about retailer. Less frequent shoppers were responsible for five times more word of mouth, because many of them exist. This pattern is typical: other retailers such as upmarket SOGO and online retailer Lazada have similar results. Any small segment equals a small effect on word-of-mouth levels, and heavy buyers are a small segment of any brand's buyer base.

An analogy would be if we thought that people with red hair give ten times more negative word of mouth because of their volatile temper. This might justify efforts to target redheads and given them extra special service to avoid their bad temper! But, as only 1–2% of the global population have red hair, the volume of negative word of mouth from this segment will be small, even at ten times more likely—hardly worth rolling out the red carpet for them! We need the incidence of people with red hair, and their contribution to the total volume of negative word of mouth, to work out if they are worth special attention. It's the same with heavy buyers: even if their propensity to buy and to give word of mouth is substantially higher, this rarely generates enough volume to compensate for their small segment size.

Any customer can give word of mouth, but for this to happen, it requires the right circumstances, such as talking to someone who asks for advice. Heavy buyers are few, which lessens the likelihood that any one of them will be in an appropriate situation to give word of mouth. Light and medium buyers are many, so it is more likely one of them will be in a situation with the opportunity to give positive word of mouth. Cultivating relationships with heavy buyers in the hope they will generate large, sustained, volumes of word of mouth is a costly distraction from the path to growth. (In Chapter 7 we talk more about word of mouth.)

Why our light buyers really matter

Our heaviest, most loyal buyers aren't a great source of growth because they are unlikely to buy much more and their low numbers don't make a major difference to the bottom line. In the case of light buyers, yes, it's the opposite, but the story is more interesting than that. Let's start with how many light buyers a brand normally has.

We (repeatedly) find that brands follow the same reverse-J shaped distribution of how many people buyer once, twice, three times and so on. This means that many infrequent buyers and a long tail of a few (very) frequent buyers. Andrew Ehrenberg first identified this in 1959 (Ehrenberg, 1959), and today we see this reverse J-shape for brands from all corners of the earth, including emerging markets. We see this distribution across countries, categories and over time. When designing a marketing strategy, this distribution is one of the most important pieces of information that any brand manager can arm themselves with.

Figure 2.1 illustrates the shape for different countries (Brazil, Philippines, Turkey), categories (toothpaste, beer and soft drinks) and

Figure 2.1: Buying frequency distributions for a range of categories, countries and brands

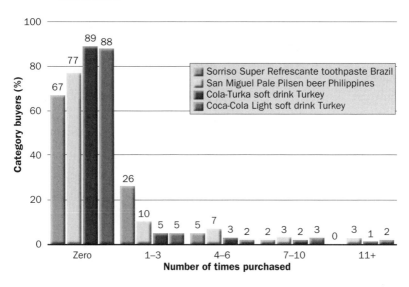

functional qualities such as local or global brands (compare Cola-Turka with Coca-Cola Light).

Larger share brands have more people buying them, and at a slightly more frequent rate (the law of double jeopardy). This law is because of this negative binomial distribution. The big potential shift in the frequency for all brands is the proportion of buyers in the zero columns, which (inversely) records each brand's penetration (see Figure 2.2). When a brand grows, the main change will usually be the zero buyer column shrinking; if the brand declines, the main change will be the zero column growing—that is, penetration will change.

Figure 2.2: Buying frequency distributions for fuel brands in the UK (2012)

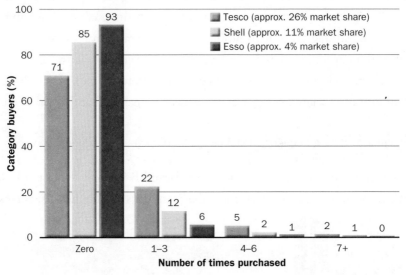

When brands grow, more light brand buyers are gained than heavy ones (see Table 2.1) and when brands decline, more light brand buyers are lost than heavy ones. In terms of influencing people, successful marketing activities therefore create more light buyers than heavy buyers. That is, we need *many* people to buy the brand once, and a *few of these* to also buy the brand again and again in the time period. By only focusing on the heavier buyers, we miss that we also need to influence the behaviour of many lighter buyers.

Table 2.1: Chinese toothpaste brand that increased by 1.5 percentage points in market share

Brand buying frequency	Year 1 (%)	Year 2 (%)	Change (Y2 – Y1)
Zero	91.7	89.8	–1.9
Once	5.0	6.3	1.3
Twice	1.6	2.0	0.4
Three times	0.7	0.8	0.2
Four times	0.6	0.5	–0.1
Five or more times	0.5	0.5	0

A brand that moves from one market share to another also moves from one negative binomial distribution to another: its new frequency chart looks rather similar to its old one. It will still have mostly light customers, a few heavy buyers, and most customers will be lighter than average. The greater a brand's penetration—that is, the more buyers it has—the more heavy buyers it has.

To illustrate this, if Brand A and Brand B have the same market share, they will usually have same amount of heavy brand buyers. But if Brand B is a smaller brand than Brand A, it will have fewer heavy buyers. This can be mistakenly interpreted to mean that Brand B is small because it lacks the heavy buyers of Brand A. Actually, Brand B is smaller because it lacks the number of customers that Brand A has in all buying weights – light, medium and heavy. Compare Tesco and Esso in Figure 2.2—Tesco has more of all types of buyers than Esso except, of course, non-buyers.

The ubiquity of this pattern means an absence of evidence that brands have succeeded by attracting or holding on to a disproportionate amount of heavy brand buyers[1].

The negative binomial distribution also gives you a crystal ball. It means you can predict your brand's (potential) future. That is, you can

---

1   This highlights the importance of correct metrics. We unfortunately see cases where consultants misinterpret metrics by only focusing on one small part of the picture.

predict the future frequency distribution of your brand, should it grow in market share. If the brand's current share is 1.5% and your objective is to become a 3% share brand, you can predict how many light, medium and heavy buyers the brand will have if it reaches 3%.

Pareto says you can't ignore light buyers

The Pareto law is usually stated as 'the top 20% of a brand's customers generate 80% of its sales'. This extreme magnitude is used to justify investments in targeting existing customers, and ignoring, or even 'firing' light buyers. But the Pareto law is not 80:20. Sharp and Romaniuk (2007) comprehensively documented the Pareto law as closer to a 50:20 pattern: that is, the top 20% of a brand's customers (the Pareto share) account for 40–60% of sales. In Table 2.2 we document additional results from a range of emerging markets to show further evidence from different countries and categories.

This law has profound strategic implications for resource allocation, just not in the way it is typically used—which is to justify concentrating resources in the very valuable customers. If 80% of a brand's customer base generated only 20% of its sales we would not be writing a chapter now on

Table 2.2: Examples of average annual brand Pareto shares across a variety of categories and countries

Country	Category	Brand's Pareto share (average)
India	Biscuits	64
Malaysia	Soft drinks	64
Philippines	Alcoholic beverages	60
Malaysia	Instant noodles	57

Country	Category	Brand's Pareto share (average)
Malaysia	Biscuits	55
Malaysia	Detergent	55
Malaysia	Bar soap	53
Malaysia	Toothpaste	51
Kenya	Soft drinks	50
Nigeria	Soft drinks	50
Indonesia	Fashion retail	49
Malaysia	Shampoo	49
Turkey	Soft drinks	49
Brazil	Toothpaste	47
China	Toothpaste	45
Mexico	Soft drinks	45
Average		**53**

the importance of light customers. This 80% could perhaps even be largely ignored. But who wants to walk away from almost half their sales?

Looking over time reveals more to this story. The Pareto share is the proportion of *this year's sales* that come from the heaviest 20% of all the people who *bought the brand this year*. And this Pareto share is usually close to being as high as 60%. But, if we track these same 'top 20' buyers next year, they will always be worth less. Some have changed their preferences, or left the country, or even died. A big driver of this is what statisticians call *regression to the mean*: over time, extremes in any cohort, such as heavy buyers, move closer to the average. In this case we can explain it very easily.

Some (but not all) of these heavy buyers really are different from most other people at least in terms of buying this brand and this category. Say the category is shampoo: perhaps they have oily hair (and need to shampoo lot) or perhaps their hair is their crowning glory, and either of these reasons means they buy the category a great deal. Coupled with this, for whatever personal reason, one brand has dominant mental and physical availability for them (perhaps it was the one their mother used?). This makes them one of the brand's very heavy users.

But other people just happened *that year* to buy the brand enough to qualify as 'heavy' (compared to other buyers). They don't usually, but this particular year they did. Many reasons are possible for this, such as an extended stay by a house guest or a fitness fad, but serendipity is a reasonable explanation. Somehow (largely unpredictable) factors came together that year that meant they bought (a bit) more than they usually do.

Yes, much 'heavy buying' is due to happenstance. Remember, it often doesn't require a huge jump in purchasing to move from being an average buyer to a heavy buyer. In many cases, even just one single additional brand purchase will do it. For example, look at Table 2.3: to move into the top 50% (the heavy half) of buyers requires only buying four times; for 16% of buyers that's just one more purchase. To move into the top 20% requires only a few more. Of course, this happens all the time. One year a buyer might buy Fanta twice, another year only once, another year four times—they are hardly likely to even notice these changes (remember four times a year is only once every three months). The buyer's ongoing propensity is to buy Fanta about twice a year, with a bit of wobble: some years more (friends' kids come to stay), some less (our kids go on away to visit relatives). What this means is that some of the people whom we thought were committed heavy buyers (because they bought us a lot in the time period we were looking at) aren't really; they just looked heavy this year, and next year it is very likely that they will buy closer to their normal rates. This will drive much of the regression to the mean.

Movement in the opposite direction is also apparent, when some of our heavier buyers will next year just happen to have a lighter than average (for them) year. Serendipity strikes again! Put this all together and we actually see that around half of the people we class as our heaviest buyers

Table 2.3: Purchase frequency distribution for Fanta in Mexico (2014)

Frequency of purchase	Buyers (%)	Cumulative %	Weight
10+ times	13	13	
9 times	1	14	Top 20%
8 times	3	17	
7 times	3	20	
6 times	7	26	
5 times	9	35	
4 times	10	45	Top 50%
3 times	16	61	
Twice	21	82	
Once	18	100	

based on a particular period of buying do not meet this criteria in the next period – and they are (perfectly) replaced by 'light buyers' who next period happen to buy at a heavy rate[2].

A relative consistency of 50% stability across brands and categories is apparent in Table 2.4, which shows the results across brands in two different categories in Malaysia[3]. About half the people who were classified as heavy buyers in one period also qualified as heavy in the subsequent period—meaning about half *weren't*.

---

2   The fact that they are perfectly replaced—that is, the number of people who drop out of the heavy buyer group is exactly matched by the number elevated into the group—seems almost magical, but of course it has to be for any brand that is stable in sales amongst these buyers. This 'magic' is because the effect is entirely statistical, due to random chance. It's the same sort of magic that allows us to make astonishingly accurate predictions about how much money casinos will take and how much they will pay out. It's the same sort of magic that allows us to predict the distribution of heights, weights, and student grades from simply knowing the average.

3   Our testing included Top 10% and classifying people by buying weight as per Romaniuk and Wight (2014). The results were consistent across heavy buyer classification approaches.

We find this level of stability applies to Western brands introduced to the country (such as Pantene, Colgate or Coca-Cola) and specialist, strongly positioned brands such as Safi, 'specifically designed to meet the need of the modern Muslim women and men' (Safi, 2015), which has around 40% heavy buyer stability in shampoo and 50% heavy buyer stability in toothpaste.

Table 2.4: Stability of heavy buyers in Malaysia (2011–12)

Soap	Top 20% stability	Noodles	Top 20% stability
Dettol Regular	47	Maggi	59
Lux	42	Cintan	49
May	29	Mamee	42
Orchid Fruitale	46	Mie Sedaap	59
Lifebuoy	30	Vits	38
Protex	37	Private Label	53
Antabax	48	Eka	42
Palmolive Naturals	34	Jasmine	42
Average	**39**		**48**

Source: Kantar WorldPanel Malaysia

This makes it hard to correctly classify heavy buyers using any snapshot of buying data, even a snapshot that covers a whole year. This rampant misclassification creates problems for any database-driven targeting of heavy customers. We risk interpreting this misclassification as indicators of success or failure of our marketing activities.

Of course we can more generally profile our customers, and it doesn't take sophisticated market research to realise that the heavy buyers of luxury European clothing brands are going to be people with a certain amount of discretionary income and an interest in fashion. But, we have to accept the following points:

- many of the people who fit this profile won't be heavy buyers of our brand (though they obviously have potential);

- that quite a lot of our heavy customers at least in a particular time period won't fit this profile
- much of our sales won't come from heavy buyers, anyway.

What about heavy category buyers?

In the quest for marketing efficiency the often-cited next question is: surely our best targets for acquisition are the heaviest buyers of the category? It's true that if these people have the highest potential they *could* buy you more often. From an efficiency or ROI perspective it probably makes sense to reach out to these customers.

In India, when Inorbit Mall opened its first Bangalore mall, no one was surprised they choose the exclusive suburb of Whitefield even if it is quite removed from the centre of the city. Inorbit Mall of course needed to be close to wealthier shoppers—people who spend more on expensive clothes and restaurants. But there were other considerations: Whitefield also has good transport infrastructure and can be reached by road, bus and rail, which is important for shoppers to shop there, and for the delivery of goods and supplies (the Container Corporation of India has a large inland container depot just off Whitefield Road).

'Fish where the fish are' can be a sound maxim. You might as well *start* where many fish are pooling together—particularly when the ocean is huge. But to grow you need to reach all sorts of category buyers—light as well as heavy. Given that a large proportion of category buyers are infrequent, even in a frequently bought category (see Figure 2.2) then they are going to be your main type of customer[4].

When a brand is small, more of its customer base is made up of heavy category buyers. Partly this is because heavy category buyers have bigger repertoires—they buy lots of brands including small ones.

---

4   It is important to avoid confusing the frequency distribution with the number of purchases or time frame or both. Over a longer time frame, everyone will buy the category more. Over a shorter time frame, everyone will buy the category less. The absolute numbers for what classifies someone as a light buyer may change, but the distribution doesn't.

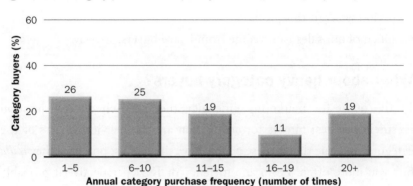

Figure 2.3: Category purchase frequency for biscuits in India (2011)

If a brand is fortunate enough to grow, then its customer base will change—a greater portion of its customers will be lighter category buyers, and a smaller portion will be heavy category buyers.

The natural monopoly law

This advantage of big brands is known as the *natural monopoly law* (Ehrenberg, 2000). Bigger brands have a greater monopoly over the light category buyers. Think of it this way – low-rating television programs are, by definition, watched by very few people. When we look at many of these programs it is rather obvious why few people would waste time watching them. More of a mystery is why anyone would, yet they do attract viewers. Who are these people watching these low-rating shows?

Well, the viewers of low-rating programs tend to be people who watch an awful lot of television. But, like all categories, the heavy television viewers are in the minority. So for a program to gain high ratings it must reach well beyond the group of heavy television viewers and attract light television viewers. This is why top-rating shows are valuable: they attract people who hardly ever watch television. This story, the natural monopoly law, is the same for brands and retailers.

To be a big brand you *must* reach out and attract many light category buyers. It's not that some big brands monopolise light category buyers and some don't—*all* attract light category buyers. If you want to be a big brand, you therefore need to attract light category buyers as well. If you want to *remain* a big brand, you need to extend your marketing activity to reach these customers, otherwise they could slip away.

This is one reason that an ROI focus can keep a brand from growing: it distracts brand managers from the main game. It seems counter-intuitive to reach out to people who don't buy the category much, and so would appear to deliver lower ROI. Ironically, focusing on ROI can prevent a brand from benefiting from scale and earning larger, more secure, profits.

Resist the seduction of sole loyalty

The chase for loyalty quickly turns into a chase for the unicorns of target marketing: the heavy category buyer who buys only your brand. While buyers can be heavy category buyers who are solely loyal to one brand, these buyers are so few that they may as well be mythical.

We illustrate this with examples from soft drinks in Turkey and Mexico (see Table 2.5), where fewer than 1% of the heaviest category buyers (buying once a day or more often) are solely loyal. Sole loyalty is highest amongst those buying once a month or less frequently; however, unfortunately fewer than 5% of category buyers buy at this rate.

Table 2.5: The relationship between category purchase frequency and sole loyalty for soft drinks in Turkey and Mexico (2014)

Purchase frequency	Turkey % solely loyal	Mexico % solely loyal
Once a day or more often	0.5	0.3
Every 2 or 3 days	0.7	0.5
Once a week	7	6
2 or 3 times a month	14	20
Once per month	29	31
Less than once a month	40	33

This might not come as a surprise for soft drink buyers—after all, it is a low-value category, prone to impulse-buying and variety-seeking by consumers. What about a completely different category, such as financial services? We find the more financial services products someone holds, the less likely they are to be solely loyal. Figure 2.4 shows how, for banks in South Africa, buyer movement from one to two products quickly halves the number of 100% loyals.

Figure 2.4: The relationship between number of products purchased and sole loyalty for financial services in South Africa (2012)

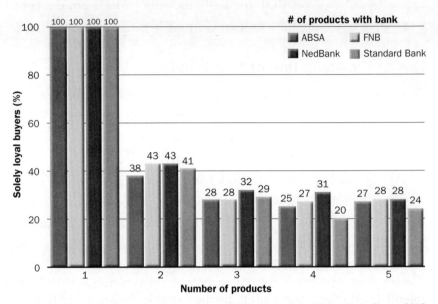

Source: National Advertising Bureau Roots Survey, 2012

To class sole-brand buying as the outcome of some deep customer intent or desire is questionable; 100% loyals are usually low-value customers who don't often buy the category. Much of what we observe as sole loyalty is happenstance, or because someone only bought the category once (and so by definition is 100% loyal to whichever brand they bought). If you extend the time frame, you see the proportion of solely loyals decline because with more opportunities to buy the category, people buy from more brands (as shown in Table 2.5).

Share loyalty (of which sole loyalty is the extreme) becomes more important for growth where it is impossible to expand the customer base. This is not a strategy to seek out but one to adapt to if the typical penetration-led path to growth is closed to the brand. The extreme idea that you should try to build a 100% loyal customer base is likely to lead to costly failure, even in subscription markets such as banking and insurance.

Sophisticated mass marketing

Marketing textbooks caricature mass marketing as offering a single marketing mix. This is nonsense. It's so silly that it's hard to think of a single real-world example. Even the Coca-Cola Company has hundreds of brands, distributed in different ways, in different places, with different advertising (in numerous languages), different prices even in the same store (cold cans are priced higher) and so on.

There is a difference between a product-range strategy and a segmentation strategy. Any successful marketer develops a product range to take into account the heterogeneity among category buyers. It's essential to do this if you want to reach all people in all buying situations (that is, target the market). But this does not require targeting specific buyers with each offer, as advocated by a segmentation strategy. Instead, a better option is for an 'anyone, anytime' sales approach. The aim is to reach everyone with a relevant, attractive, offer in as many buying situations as possible, without generating over-the-top complexity and destroying scale advantages. The secret to doing this is to look for commonalities, and mass ways of reaching customers both physically and mentally.

Customers do vary a great deal in their lifestyles, interests, wealth, age and so on. It is easy to get distracted by these differences and to make things more complicated than they need be. The customer differences that matter, that are of any practical value, should be very obvious (for example, geographic differences); if they are not, they are unlikely to matter.

Sophisticated mass marketers can offer a great deal of customisation without having to identify and target different buyers. For example, a great deal of customisation occurs at the point of sale, where buyers choose between options for a number of different characteristics:

- payment
- delivery
- packaging
- volume of the order
- insurance, and so on.

This sort of customisation is offered to all customers and is not based on identifying particular types of people and targeting them. Customers are allowed individual expression, and vote with their wallet.

Don't shoot yourself with target marketing

Contrary to popular belief, target marketing is not clever. Nor is it customer-centric. Like salt in cooking, a little bit of targeting makes sense but tighter targeting than targeting category buyers is a recipe for negative growth.

The desire to target just a fraction of the market is often based on the idea that the brand is highly differentiated and so must appeal to some and not others—or that it must be made to (because Kotler or Aaker told me so). Data on real-world buying just does not support this view (see *How Brands Grow*, Chapter 5, and award-winning research such as Kennedy & Ehrenberg, 2001; Kennedy, Ehrenberg & Long, 2000; Uncles et al., 2012). Rival brands sell to highly similar customer bases, each made up of a very similar mixture of heterogeneous buyers. The stark difference is that some brands have bigger customer bases than others.

A really dangerous practice in modern marketing is to describe a market as a single person: for example, 'our target consumer is Nicole, she's 28 years old, is passionate about the environment and sustainability, shops at Whole Foods market, likes new experiences, reads classic literature but also watches *Keeping up with the Kardashians* as a guilty pleasure'. This is the height of inane target marketing: to treat all those very different customers as if they are clones of Nicole. In defence, some will say this caricature is just to 'bring the customer alive', to 'help thinking', but it is lazy, dangerous thinking that often finds its way into advertising and media plans, and the brand ends up talking only to a tiny fraction of its potential market. Many new brands have failed to generate enough sales to justify their existence, not because they were bad products, but because this sort of targeting guaranteed that they would undershoot their sales targets. A large share of a tiny (Nicole) market still equals very low sales.

America's biggest Hispanic-owned food company, Goya Foods, began in 1936 as a specialty distributor of basic products, such as beans, to Hispanic immigrants. Today it is one of the USA's fastest-growing food companies, introducing all sorts of Americans to a (wide) range of Hispanic-inspired food items. 'We like to say we don't market to Latinos, we market as Latinos', says CEO Bob Unanue (Wentz, 2013). In the UK, the brand Quorn offers a wide range of meat-free protein dishes. They could have targeted vegetarians, as these are the people for whom the brand had the most obvious appeal. Instead, as they explain, 'We started to transform the brand's positioning from a vegetarian substitute (relevant to around 7% of UK households) to a broader healthy eating brand (relevant to around 70% of UK households), thus opening up a significantly larger penetration led growth opportunity'. By the end of 2011 Quorn were responsible for delivering 62% of category growth with sales up £6.8 million (Wragg & Regan, 2012).

Goya Foods and Quorn are examples of marketers thinking about the category needs their brands could satisfy, and worrying less about who within the category is going to buy their brand. This thinking widened their potential markets and created sales opportunities that would have been missed if they had stuck to their 'target' markets.

Conclusion

This chapter explained why light buyers matter most, and the importance of sophisticated mass marketing to build a large brand. Most growth will come from light and non-buyers of the brand, simply because of how many of them there are, and the room they have to increase their purchasing. The natural monopoly law also highlights the importance of designing marketing strategies that reach out to light category buyers.

We also exposed many of the loyalty and targeting fallacies that are peddled to marketers. Next we look at what other brands your customers buy, and what can be learnt from this.

3

Where New Customers Come From

Byron Sharp and Jenni Romaniuk

We've seen that, to grow, a brand needs to recruit new buyers and encourage very light buyers to favour the brand a little more. This means winning buyers from other brands, which raises the question of which other brands' customers we should target.

We showcase a law-like pattern that makes managing a brand a little less complicated. Insightfully examining differences between brands' customer bases leads to the realisation that your brand potentially competes with every other brand in the category, for the same customers. While this might at first seem daunting, we show how to use this knowledge to your advantage.

Then we turn to what can be learnt by monitoring the competitors' brands bought by your consumers. We show how to systematically analyse the competitive structure of the market, from different viewpoints (for example, brand, product type, price point or region).

Today's markets can have all sorts of variation, which need to be understood in order to manage a portfolio of brands. The key to getting a handle on this complexity is to first understand the pattern of brand switching or sharing to expect. The *duplication of purchase* law provides this baseline.

Competitive brands have similar customer bases

If positioning-based targeting actually worked, we would see rival brands each selling to different types of customers. But this rarely turns out to be the case. When we compare the customer profiles of competing brands, they look strikingly similar (Hammond, Ehrenberg & Goodhardt, 1996; Kennedy & Ehrenberg, 2001; Kennedy, Ehrenberg & Long, 2000; Uncles et al., 2012). Evidence continues to build for brands in emerging markets with very low variation evident in countries as diverse as Turkey, India and China (Truong, Faulkner & Mueller Loose, 2012; Uncles et al., 2012).

For example, if we look at the South Korean fast food market (Table 3.1), and compare brand-user profiles for ten of the top brands, we see that the average brand's customer base is about half male (48%); about a sixth of customers (15%) are aged 18–24 years; about a third of buyers (34%) are lower income and so on. Also immediately apparent, when you look at the data in this way, is how similar this story is for every brand. Lotteria, a large local chain selling burgers, has 47% male customers, similar to McDonald's (52% male) and so on—all very close to half. The variance, quantified in the mean absolute deviation, is between 1 and 3 percentage points. We also see very little difference in the user profiles of local and global brands: competing brands sell to similar customers.

South Korea's results are not unusual. We see this pattern play out in fast food across the world, as illustrated by Table 3.2 which shows the

Table 3.1: Fast food in South Korea eaten in the last six months—sample of demographic profiles

Brands (in penetration order)	Male (%)	18–24 years (%)	25–34 years (%)	Lower income (%)	Higher income (%)	Have children aged under 5 (%)	One person in household (%)	Work full time (%)
*Lotteria	47	16	25	37	16	13	8	62
McDonald's	52	16	28	35	17	13	8	67
KFC	51	13	29	35	18	10	9	68
Pizza Hut	48	14	22	31	20	12	6	69
*Paris Baguette	46	15	24	36	14	11	9	63
Dunkin' Donuts	46	15	27	33	20	14	6	66
Domino's pizza	44	13	29	33	20	16	7	72
*Tour Les Jour	42	18	25	35	15	15	7	63
Burger King	53	16	29	31	21	11	6	66
*Kyochon	50	16	18	31	19	14	7	70
Average	48	15	26	34	18	13	7	67
Mean absolute deviation	**3**	**1**	**3**	**2**	**2**	**2**	**1**	**3**
Average (local brands only)	**46**	**16**	**23**	**35**	**16**	**13**	**8**	**64**

*Local brand

mean absolute deviations for key demographic variables across eleven emerging markets, ranging from China to Mexico to Nigeria.

Fast food brands largely compete for the same type of customers. Over more than 3000 cross-tabulations involving more than 100 brands, only 2.5% of brands deviated more than 10 percentage points from the average brand on that characteristic, even though the brands sell very different types of food (including local cuisine, chicken, hamburgers, pizza and doughnuts).

Table 3.2: Mean absolute deviations (in percentage points) in fast food brand-user profiles across eleven countries

Country	Gender	Age	Household size (number of people)	Children at home	Work status	Income
Brazil	3*	3	2	3	5	3
China	5	3	2	3	1	4
India	2	3	2	3	2	2
Indonesia	4	2	2	2	2	2
Kenya	3	4	2	3	3	3
Mexico	3	3	2	2	3	2
Nigeria	4	3	2	2	2	2
Russia	6	3	2	2	3	3
South Africa	3	2	3	2	3	4
South Korea	5	4	2	2	3	2
Turkey	2	3	2	3	2	3
Category average MAD	4	3	2	3	3	3

*Interpreted as, for example, fast food brands in Brazil varied in the percentage of males from the average brand by 3 percentage points—so if the average brand had 50% in its customer base, brands are between 47% and 53%.

What about service categories?

Similarity in customer profiles extends to categories such as financial services, telecommunications and insurance. Table 3.3 shows the results for personal banking in seven countries. While we see larger variation between providers than we saw for fast food, particularly for income and work status variables, much of this variation is easily explainable.

Table 3.3: Mean absolute deviation variation (in percentage points) in banks' customer profiles (2014)

Country	Gender	Age	Household size (number of people)	Work status	Income
Brazil	3	4	3	6	4
China	4	3	2	2	3
India	3	3	3	3	3
Indonesia	3	4	2	3	7
Russia	5	3	4	4	3
South Africa	3	2	2	4	6
South Korea	4	3	2	3	3
Category average	4	3	3	4	4

Let's dive a little deeper into the two countries with larger differences in the income levels of their banking customers: Indonesia and South Africa.

For Indonesia, the deviations were evident in foreign banks that had disproportionately more customers with monthly incomes over 7 million rupiah (Citibank, +17 percentage points; HSBC, +20 percentage points; Standard Chartered, +22 percentage points; ANZ, +14 percentage points) and several local banks having fewer higher income customers (for example: BRI, –18 percentage points; BNI, –12 percentage points; BTN, –12 percentage points).

In South Africa, specific brands drive the variation. Postbank, which is a bank operated out of the South African Post Office, has more low-income customers (+29 percentage points), while Investec, an international specialist investment bank and asset manager, is a mirror image with more higher income customers (+36 percentage points). The sources of the differences are thus unsurprising, and based on the functional differences between the brands: that is, the range of services they provide, their fees and where they have branches.

Before we wrap up discussion of this law-like pattern regarding the similarity of the customer profiles of competing brands, let's look at one more category: telecommunications. Growth in mobile phone usage means that telecommunications is becoming an increasingly important category in emerging markets. Often this category is just emerging from government regulation and opening up to foreign companies.

With many countries having only a few very large providers, the scene might be set for more specific targeting of customers as these competitors slice up the market. But, as Table 3.4 shows, we find across eight countries that, again, the user profiles of competitive brands differ very little, with mean average deviations of around 3 percentage points. In only 4% of cases, brands differed by more than 10 percentage points from the category average.

Table 3.4: Mean average deviation variations (in percentage points) in telecommunication services' customer profiles (2014)

Country	Gender	Age	Household size (number of people)	Age of children	Income
Brazil	2	4	2	5	3
India	4	3	1	3	2
Indonesia	2	5	4	3	3
Mexico	5	4	3	5	4
Nigeria	6	4	3	5	4
Russia	4	2	3	3	3
South Africa	2	1	1	2	2
Turkey	1	2	1	2	2
Category average	3	3	2	3	3

Loyal switchers

Your customers are much the same as other brands' customers. One reason for this similarity is that your customers also buy other brands. The customers who return to your store or repeat-buy your brand also buy your competitors' brands. This is a fundamental fact of competitive markets.

It is not uncommon for a brand manager to look at their Kantar or Nielsen report and, when they see that their customers only devote, say, a third of all their annual purchasing to their brand, exclaim with dismay 'my customers buy other brands most of the time'. They might then try to craft strategies to build up share loyalty. But such customer behaviour is normal. In the famous words of Andrew Ehrenberg, 'your customers are really other people's customers who occasionally buy you'.

In subscription markets, buyers allocate a large portion of their category buying to one brand: for example, we usually only have only one hairdresser and only one dentist (Sharp, Wright & Goodhardt, 2002). But, over time and purchase occasions, people have repertoires. Service firms offer many different products and services, but their customers seldom buy all of these from the same provider. Consequently even a bank or an insurance provider may typically find that only around half of its customers consider that bank their main institution: many of their customers are largely another bank's customer (see Figure 3.1 for examples from Indonesia and South Korea). This is especially the case for smaller banks shown in Figure 3.1, such as Permata, the tenth-biggest bank in Indonesia, which is the main financial institution for only 15% of its customers, or Hana Bank in South Korea, which has only 26% of its customers say it is their main institution.

Nowadays, particularly in emerging markets, it is not unusual to have multiple phone handsets as well as SIM cards from multiple providers to take advantage of the different offers from telecommunications providers. Some people, when they hear this, throw their arms in the air and say 'there is no loyalty any more'. This is very wrong, on two counts. Firstly, nothing has changed; this is how your grandparents, and their grandparents,

Figure 3.1: Percentage of bank customers with that bank as their main financial institution in (a) Indonesia and (b) South Korea (2014)

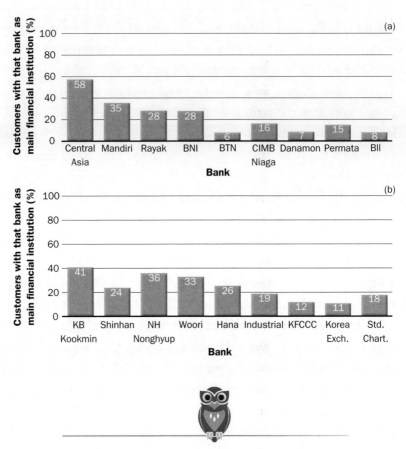

bought brands. No past golden age of loyalty existed where people each bought only one brand religiously (except perhaps as a fairytale written in marketing textbooks). Secondly, while people buy from a repertoire, they are also very loyal: brands are not bought randomly. Loyalty appears to be a natural human behaviour (Livaditis, Sharp & Sharp, 2012; Sharp, 2013, pp. 38–41).

While people are not 100% loyal, this does not mean we need to jump to the opposite extreme and disclaim any loyalty. We see that not everyone who bought a category twice will have bought two brands—in fact, a good proportion will have bought the same brand twice. The pattern continues: people who bought three times bought fewer than three brands; people who bought four times bought fewer than four brands and so on.

If you look at the heaviest buyers, over a long time period, or at a category where people buy very frequently, like noodles, then some buyers have bought the category a great deal but their repertoire size, or the number of brands they actually bought, will be remarkably small. People keep returning to the same brands.

In Figure 3.2, we see two clear patterns from a South Korean alcoholic beverage category with more than 50 brands. The first is that as category purchase frequency increases, so does the number of brands bought (repertoire size). The second is that as category purchase frequency increases, the repertoire size as a percentage of category purchase frequency declines—signalling that the more people purchase a category, the more they tend to go back to the same brands to fulfil these additional purchases.

Figure 3.2: The relationship between (a) category purchase frequency and (b) repertoire size for alcoholic spirits in South Korea (2012)

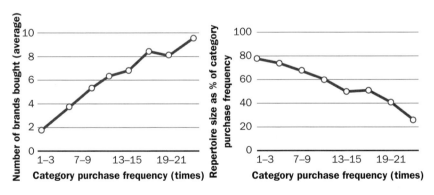

People are naturally loyal, yet it isn't normal for them to behave in either of these ways:

- buy only one brand over many purchase occasions; or
- buy a different brand for every purchase occasion.

Reality lies, somewhat unglamorously, somewhere in the middle of these two extremes.

Using predictable customer overlap

Your customers (and potential customers) buy other brands; indeed, they may mostly buy other brands. The *duplication of purchase* law predicts how many of your customers will buy each other competitive brand within any time period. Stated simply, the duplication of purchase law says that brands will share their customers in line with the other brands' penetration.

- A brand bought by most people in the market will also be bought by most of your customers.
- A brand that is bought by very few people in the market will be bought by few of your customers.

Put like this the duplication of purchase law sounds rather intuitive[1], but what's surprising is its precision. It predicts that each brand will have a consistent level of customer overlap with all other competitive brands. The level of this overlap will also be correlated with the brand's share. A larger brand will have a higher overlap with all other brands than a smaller brand. This means that *if*, in a particular time period, 20% of all the people who bought fuel at Shell in the UK also bought from BP, *then* 20% of customers from other fuel retailers will also have bought from BP.

The duplication of purchase law says that competitive overlap, or the degree of competitive clout that a brand has over another, depends primarily on the brand's size. This also suggests that competition is largely about mental and physical availability, and not brand positioning, history, quality and so on.

Knowing that this pattern is the norm allows us to spot exceptions (referred to as *partitions*) that can provide additional insights and

---

1   It has been referred to as 'fair share' and other terms, but this is often meant as a possible outcome rather than an empirical law.

opportunities. But before we do that, we will show how to reveal the predictable patterns of customer overlap in a simple table.

A duplication of purchase table shows the degree to which brands within a category share their buyers with each of the other brands in the category (that is, what proportion of their customers also bought another particular brand during the period). Table 3.5 is a duplication of purchase table with no data.

Table 3.5: Duplication of purchase (no data)

Brand	% buying	Buyers who also bought other brands (%)			
		A	B	C	D
A	Highest	100%			
B	...		100%		
C	...			100%	
D	Lowest				100%

The 100% cells are a brand's level of customer overlap with itself, which logically must be 100%. In terms of the presentation of the data, it is good practice to blank out these cells, because they will distract from the key patterns, as well as distort the column averages.

Duplication of purchase tables refer to a particular time period: for example, the people during the year who bought brand A and who also bought brand B. Note that a buyer of brand A needs to only make one purchase of brand B to be counted. Consequently, duplication analyses that apply to very long periods can be misleading, because every brand may show very high levels of sharing with every other brand. This obscures who competes more or less closely.

At the other end of the time spectrum, little duplication occurs in very short time periods, because most customers only bought the category once. This is also misleading. The analyst should choose a period long enough to capture a degree of repeated purchase: that is, a period long enough to allow most people to have revealed their repertoire of multiple brands.

Fortunately, this is usually easy—the analyses aren't overly sensitive to the time period outside the two extremes mentioned.

Readers of duplication tables need to note that they refer to a particular period, rather than an absolute metric; one can't simply say, '20% of Shell shoppers also buy fuel at BP'; it's 20% *in a month* or *in a year*.

A duplication of purchase table from annual purchases in the haircare category in China (Table 3.6) shows customer overlap in this time period varies from about two-thirds of every brand sharing customers with Pantene, down to less than a fifth sharing with Clear, the smallest brand in the table.

With the brands ordered by declining penetration, the duplication of purchase law becomes easy to see. Every brand shares more of its customers with larger competitors, and less with smaller competitors. It is also apparent just how accurate the duplication of purchase law is in this market; the brand scores running down the columns are very close to one another (and to the average) in spite of all the things going on in the market in that year (promotions, new SKU launches, natural disasters, marketing mistakes)—and, of course, sampling error on any market research sample.

Now that we can see the duplication of purchase law so clearly, we can also spot a few partitions. These would be difficult without arranging the data like this, or knowing about the duplication of purchase law. Four figures are emphasised, to make them easy to see. Rejoice DC and Rejoice Essence share customers with each other more than expected, as do Clear and Lux. In both of these cases, these are brands marketed by the same company, a common reason for higher-than-expected customer overlap.

Table 3.6: Duplication of purchase table for haircare in China (200*)

Buyers of	Buyers buying brand (%)	Buyers also buying in 2008 (%)										
		Pantene	H & S	Rejoice DC	Lux	Bang Wang	Slek	Vidal Sassoon	Rejoice Ess.	Clairol	Hazeline	Clear
Pantene	54		56	39	38	27	31	27	28	29	28	17
H & S	49	60		38	34	26	30	26	30	27	28	17
Rejoice DC	33	64	57		39	29	32	28	53	30	30	16
Lux	31	66	55	41		28	35	33	30	31	33	23
Bang Wang	26	55	49	37	34		31	25	27	23	23	16
Slek	26	64	57	41	42	31		28	32	28	35	17
Vidal Sassoon	23	63	54	40	43	28	31		28	38	31	18
Rejoice Ess.	23	64	63	75	39	30	35	28		32	31	16
Clairol	23	66	58	42	42	25	31	39	32		35	20
Hazeline	23	65	61	42	43	26	39	32	32	35		16
Clear	14	64	61	38	51	30	31	31	28	34	27	
Average	30	63	57	43	40	28	32	30	32	31	30	18

Source: Faulkner, Truong & Romaniuk, 2014

Take the McDonald's challenge

Let us take a look at how brands compete within a category with quite a number of functional differences: fast food. Before you look at Table 3.7, have a think about the major brands you know, and how they might share customers. Where might partitions lie? Would you expect McDonald's and Burger King to attract people who like burgers, and so share customers more than expected? Or perhaps because these brands offer a similar product range, a consumer only needs one in their repertoire to satisfy that feel-like-a-burger moment? What about Pizza Hut and Domino's? Would you expect them to share more or fewer customers than expected?

It would be easy to craft a credible story to support possibilities of both higher and lower sharing between brands. But the data tells us we would be wrong in both cases. Actually McDonald's and Burger King share customers in line with the duplication of purchase law predictions, and so do Pizza Hut and Domino's. Indeed McDonald's and Domino's also share customers in line with expectations, as do Pizza Hut and Burger King (see Table 3.7). The major partition (highlighted) is between Vips and Sanborns, who both only offer cafeteria-style local cuisine.

Apart from this exception, fast food retailers in Mexico share customers with other retailers in line with the competitors' penetration. Everyone shares more customers with Burger King (a big brand) and fewer customers with Gorditas Dona Tota (a much smaller brand), irrespective of the specific food they sell. This is how we expect a normal competitive market to look.

Before we get too involved with the exceptions, let's remember what this law-like pattern in competition means for growth. If Chili's wants to grow to double in size, it will have to look like Pizza Hut. We don't mean it will start selling pizzas but it will have many more people buying it, and the sales it will steal will come mainly from the larger competitors (Burger King, Domino's) and to a lesser degree from the smaller brands (Sanborns, Gorditas Dona Tota). It is not about targeting a specific competitor but drawing customers from all brands, in proportion to their share.

Table 3.7: Duplication of purchase table for fast food in Mexico (2014)

Customers of	Customers buying brand (%)	Customers also buying in six-month period (%)									
		Burger King	Domino's	KFC	McDonald's	Subway	Pizza Hut	Vips	Sanborns	Chili's	Gorditas Dona Tota
Burger King	56		65	63	62	61	52	46	42	28	16
Domino's	54	66		64	66	59	58	46	40	27	16
KFC	52	67	67		63	57	56	44	38	28	17
McDonald's	51	68	70	64		60	55	44	37	30	15
Subway	46	74	69	65	66		55	49	43	32	17
Pizza Hut	42	69	75	70	67	61		47	44	29	14
Vips	35	74	71	66	65	65	57		61	37	18
Sanborns	30	78	72	66	63	65	61	70		40	19
Chili's	20	76	72	72	75	73	59	63	59		20
Gorditas Dona Tota	13	72	71	70	60	63	48	49	45	33	
Average	40	72	70	67	65	63	56	51	45	32	17

Insights from partitions

The duplication of purchase law gives us the benchmarks to identify when brands share more or fewer customers than they should. Clusters of over-sharing and under-sharing partitions are usually easy to spot. As a rule of thumb we look for 10 percentage points difference from average, but this is just a guide. The first partitions to note are those with deviations on both sides of the diagonal (such as in the case of Sanborns and Vips in Table 3.7). But the occasional, one-sided deviations are also worth noting as they can suggest marketing shortfalls.

Finding explanations for these partitions can help identify what features are important to consumers, highlight problems to correct or uncover market opportunities. Let's look at the soft drink category in Turkey. Again, this is a category with a number of functional differences (diet drinks, fruit flavoured, colas), some positioning differences (Cola-Turka marketing itself as the brand that makes you more Turkish), plus a combination of local (Uludag, Yedigun) and global brands (Coca-Cola, Pepsi, Sprite).

With many possibilities for slicing and dicing the market, let's first use a duplication of purchase table (Table 3.8) to find the excess or deficits in sharing—and uncover what brand characteristics really make a demonstrative difference to the behaviour of buyers.

First, does nationalism matter? Looking at Table 3.8, it would seem a little bit, but not much. Cola-Turka and Coca-Cola share slightly fewer customers than average, but still 72% of Cola-Turka's drinkers also drank Coca-Cola in the last three months—not really that different from the average of 80%.

Second, does diet matter? We can see that the diet soft drinks (Coca-Cola light, Coke Zero, Pepsi Light) all share customers more than expected, so it seems this is an important functional difference. Therefore it might be prudent for all companies to ensure they have a diet version to compete in that partition. Not doing so would restrict penetration a little, as the brand would fail to tap into some buying situations.

Third, does brand name matter? We see that Pepsi Light shares more customers than it should with Pepsi (73% versus an average of 59%) but

Table 3.8: Duplication of purchase table for soft drinks in Turkey (2014)

Buyers of	Buyers buying brand (%)	Buyers also buying in last three months (%)												
		Coca-Cola	Fanta	Uludag	Pepsi	Yedigünw	Sprite	Çamlica	Sirma	Cola-Turka	Coca-Cola light	Coke Zero	7up	Pepsi Light
Coca-Cola	70		59	48	52	40	43	38	29	17	19	16	12	11
Fanta	52	79		55	55	57	47	45	35	23	20	14	14	12
Uludag	45	75	64		53	55	48	58	37	24	20	15	14	12
Pepsi	44	83	65	54		54	47	45	34	25	22	15	15	16
Yedigün	38	75	79	65	63		50	55	36	28	21	15	18	14
Sprite	37	82	66	59	56	51		53	41	23	25	19	21	14
Çamlica	36	74	65	73	55	58	55		44	31	20	15	18	14
Sirma	26	76	69	62	56	51	57	59		28	28	21	19	16
Cola-Turka	17	**72**	73	65	66	63	50	67	44		30	17	18	23
Coca-Cola light	16	83	65	57	61	50	57	44	46	31		**41**	19	**41**
Coke Zero	14	83	53	50	48	41	50	39	41	20	**47**		18	**32**
7up	10	82	75	63	65	67	80	63	52	30	30	25		20
Pepsi Light	10	83	68	56	73	56	55	53	44	40	**68**	**47**	21	
Average	**26**	**80**	**66**	**60**	**59**	**54**	**55**	**54**	**42**	**28**	**26**	**18**	**18**	**16**

the reverse is not the case, whereby 16% of Pepsi customers also buy Pepsi Light, which is as expected. This is most likely due to an issue with physical availability. Pepsi Light, being a small brand, probably has incomplete distribution. Where it is distributed, it will usually sit right by Pepsi, thereby causing what looks like excess cannibalisation. PepsiCo should aim to fix the distribution shortfall, and then the sharing should revert to normal (similar to Coca-Cola, Coca-Cola light and Coke Zero). Shared brand names rarely result in a deviation from the duplication of purchase law except in the case of a small, poorly distributed sibling brand. This is something to be rectified rather than celebrated.

Are local brands a separate sub-market?

Throughout the history of globalisation research, local brands have been a source of intense interest. Initially, it was thought they would suffer, and be perceived as poorer quality than their global counterparts. Now people, given the success of some local brands in emerging markets, have performed a 180-degree turn, and speculate that local brands will command higher brand loyalty because of nationalistic sentiments.

As illustrated by the two examples here (fast food in Mexico and soft drinks in Turkey—Tables 3.7 and 3.8) where both local and global brands are present, no local or global brand partition exists. Nor, from earlier in the chapter, do we see evidence that local brands sell to a different profile of buyer. That is, no one specifically buys (or doesn't buy) local brands. Local brands compete in the same market as every other brand. Whether you should fear or ignore them is directly related to their current market share.

On occasion we see deviations for local brands but, as previously mentioned, these tend to be a by-products of patchy (often regional) distribution. In countries as large and diverse as China and India, where economies have been relatively sheltered from global markets historically, the presence of strong regional players is unsurprising. Whether these regional brands can become strong national brands is a different issue. Our advice would be always when you see a brand acting differently, first look for explanations in incomplete distribution or functional differences.

Only after these two explanations have been excluded should you explore more esoteric explanations such as brand positioning or differentiation.

Conclusion

To grow, your brand needs to attract new customers. This means gaining customers from competitors, and this chapter sheds light as to which ones. Understanding how brands compete, so you don't get distracted by less important competition, need not be complicated. We have some simple empirical laws that hold in a wide range of markets to help us make sense of even complex, many layered, categories. Remember these key facts:

- the profile of your brand's customer base should follow that of the category profile. If it doesn't, find out why your market is restricted, and fix it if you can.
- expect that your brand's major competition will be larger share brands, unless you have empirical evidence to tell you otherwise.
- if you grow, you most likely will take sales from all brands, in proportion to their current share, so don't be distracted by positioning claims or even functional differences on the path to growth—sometimes these matter, but often less than you imagine.
- use partition analysis to make sure you are playing in the whole market, and not locking the brand out of key subcategories because you don't offer a suitable variant. Look for and, if possible, eradicate these barriers to penetration growth.

4

Building Mental Availability

Jenni Romaniuk

In prior chapters we explained why brands, even in complex, high involvement, intangible categories, compete largely for mental and physical availability. Growth depends on building these two market-based assets at a faster rate than competitors. In this chapter we take an in-depth look at mental availability, explain which memory structures the brand should prioritise and explore why persistent refreshment of these brand memories is important for ongoing success.

We also update long-held ideas about the consideration set and brand positioning in light of current knowledge about buyer memory and behaviour.

The brand = our memories

Appearances can be deceiving. Even in our most blank and distracted moments, we have a lot going on in our brains. Unfortunately, your brain can be like an unreliable friend, like the one who offers to meet you at 7 p.m. and turns up at 8 p.m., or tells you another beer is the best cure for a hangover. Our brain notices what it notices, and that may depend more on millions of years of evolution, and years of exposures, than useful direction from our conscious mind. For example it would be useful for me to commit to memory the name of that new conditioner that will tame frizzy hair once and for all, but all that comes to mind is that Penelope Cruz was in the advertisement and I saw her last in *Vicky Cristina Barcelona*. Nothing particularly useful for my current or future hair!

When we encounter a brand, we *may* generate thoughts and feelings about that experience. When we do, brand memory structures develop and these memories are at the centre of a brand's equity.

Brands pop into our daily lives in many ways:

- using, consuming or buying
- seeing other people use or buy
- seeing advertising
- seeing a branded delivery truck
- interacting with the brand on social media
- reading or hearing about it from someone—a friend or spokesperson.

Each such encounter potentially affects our brain by refreshing existing brand memories or creating new ones. This brain activity *can* build a brand's mental availability. The use of *may* and *can* when talking about the effect of an exposure on buyers' memories is deliberate. Exposure alone is not enough to guarantee the type of imprint typically sought from marketing activities—but it's a start. Without exposure, there is no chance of building mental availability.

We all have similar brains

One human brain works largely in the same way as another. Yes, some of us are better at maths and others at dancing but, in the absence of a cognitive impairment, our brains work in a similar way (just as human eyes, ears and feet work in much the same way). Country or culture doesn't matter very much[1]—neurosurgeons don't need to know what country you are from in order to perform brain surgery.

But our life experiences create our memories, which means we all hold different stuff in our brains. Neuroscientist Susan Greenfield calls memory our 'personalisation' of the brain (Greenfield 2000). *How* a brand is encoded, stored and retrieved from buyer memory is similar across buyers but *what* our memories contain varies to reflect our own encounters with categories and brands. Across different markets, buyers may therefore contain or prioritise different memories about the category and its brands.

Memory affects buying; buying affects memory

A stark empirical fact is that we know more about brands we buy and we buy the brands we know more about. We rarely buy brands we don't know and rarely think about brands we don't buy. One of the most well-established scientific laws about brand associations reflects this: brand users are more likely to elicit associations than non-users of the brand.

This pattern was documented in the 1960s by Andrew Ehrenberg and colleagues (Bird & Channon, 1969; Bird, Channon & Ehrenberg, 1970). Forty years later, Romaniuk, Bogomolova and Dall'Olmo Riley (2012) showed this law continues to hold in a wide range of categories and countries, including emerging markets, durables and services (see Table 4.1). Indeed the effect of buying a brand lingers long after ceasing the behaviour, as we can see that former buyers are more likely to give positive associations than those who have never bought the brand.

---

1   Studies emphasising the differences between brains of different cultures, such as Tang and colleagues (2006), tend to focus on preferences for visual versus audio information rather than *how* visual and audio information are processed.

Table 4.1: Brand associations for buyers and non-buyers across different countries and categories, selected from Romaniuk, Bogomolova and Dall'Olmo Riley (2012)

Countries	Current buyers (%)	Former buyer (%)	Never bought (%) (all results)
South Korea	36	31	23
India	77	28	16
Brazil	44	13	7
Russia	50	20	9
Turkey	39	10	5
China	30	15	4
Categories			
Business banking	50	20	17
Personal banking	52	15	10
Financial advisers	43	33	11
Supermarket retailers	37	18	8
Fast food retail	34	22	8
Average (all)	**48**	**19**	**10**
Average (Bird, Channon & Ehrenberg, 1970)	**50**	**20**	**10**

This tendency for buyers to give more responses translates to bigger brands (with more buyers) usually scoring higher on associations than small brands. For example, Table 4.2 shows responses to 'good as a gift', for buyers and non-buyers for whisky brands in a mature (the UK) and an emerging (South Africa) whisky market. Buyers of each brand consistently

Table 4.2: Percentage response to 'good as a gift' for the same whisky brands across two markets (2010)

Brands	South Africa		United Kingdom	
	Buyer %	Non-Buyer %	Buyer %	Non-Buyer %
Jack Daniels	53	31	61	24
Bells	28	20	40	15
Grants	23	10	33	15
Average	**35**	**20**	**45**	**18**

give more associations than non-buyers: a rule of thumb is about two to three times in favour of buyers.

Surprisingly, even what could be considered negative attributes often follow this pattern (Winchester & Romaniuk, 2008), as seen in Table 4.3 for the attribute 'expensive' across soft drink brands in Turkey and Mexico. The perception of 'expensive' and many other negative associations is not just negative, but also descriptive or factual. More buyers know this fact than non-buyers. Buyer experience develops associations and opinions about a brand, whether these associations are positive or negative. Later in the chapter we discuss the fallacy of brand rejection driving most non-buying.

Table 4.3: Associations with 'expensive' for soft drink brands in Turkey and Mexico (2014)

Brands (in average market share order)	Turkey		Mexico	
	Buyer (%)	Non-buyer (%)	Buyer (%)	Non-buyer (%)
Coca-Cola	43	39	62	50
Pepsi	16	14	22	15
Sprite	17	10	11	7
Fanta	14	9	8	7
Average	23	18	26	20

Our brain when buying

Let's first look at the basic architecture of the brand in the brain, and how we encode, store, and access the memories it contains. Then we can use the way the brain works to influence it on our brand's behalf.

The *associative network theories* (ANT) are a commonly accepted group of theories of memory that share common foundations (for more detail, see Anderson & Bower, 1979). These foundations include that memories consist of nodes. When encountered together, these nodes can form links (become *associated*). For example, if someone sees an advertisement with

David Beckham and Adidas, they might form a link between 'David Beckham' and 'Adidas' in their memory (Adidas would certainly hope so—they paid a great deal of money for that endorsement!). Then seeing David Beckham during a World Cup broadcast creates a small chance that the person thinks of Adidas, which might help Adidas if he or she is shopping for sports shoes at that time.

Types of memory

We often think of memory as being like a library. When we need to recall a memory we metaphorically trundle off to the library (search our brains) and retrieve the book (memory) we were looking for. This metaphor distracts us from the fact that we are accessing memories continuously, in real time, at lightning speed. These are some of the most common types of memory we use every waking second, often without paying any conscious attention:

- *semantic memory* is our memory for words and their meaning, such as knowledge that Singapore is a place; that noodles are a food; and Koka is a brand of instant noodle. We draw on this knowledge for reasoning and solving problems.
- *episodic memory* is our memory for events, such as the last time we went out to a particular restaurant to celebrate a birthday. Many events start out as episodic memories and then get integrated into semantic memory over time as the events get become part of our general memory structure.
- *implicit memory* includes our memory for processes. Implicit memory often directs our behaviour when we are on autopilot, such as when driving a car after many years of experience. This includes many brand choices when doing everyday shopping.
- *sensory memory* is our memory for smells, sounds, sights and touch, such as the al dente texture when we eat pasta. Sensory memories may be powerful in the moment, but fade quickly.

Memories help us navigate the day. They helped me to physically type this paragraph, without having to consciously think about every keystroke (implicit), to recall past events for examples (episodic), and to make sure the right words were used in the right places (semantic).

Our memory for brands

For a small part of any day, we are buyers of brands and audiences for marketing activities. It's easy to exaggerate how long this is but, for most buyers on most days, buying (including thinking about buying) takes up little time and (ideally) little effort. When we buy, we draw on a subset of our memory to help make each choice. The thoughts and actions of buying are typically these:

- instantaneous, without (much) conscious deliberation
- influenced by context, which defines which part of memory is triggered
- inconsistent, in that today's retrieved thoughts are not necessarily retrieved tomorrow.

When buying, we search our memory for a reason: which is to identify something to buy, for *that* situation. This is quite different from, say, completing a school test; buyers are not seeking to generate a list of brands in a category. Buyers use specific thoughts to access relevant answers. This process is referred to as *cued retrieval* (for more on this, see Tulving & Craik, 2000).

Cued retrieval

What we (easily) think of largely determines what we buy, so what determines what we (easily) think of in a particular instant? First, the doorway or *cue* used to access memory matters, as this determines the possible paths your thoughts can travel down. Open the green door, and you travel down one path in memory; open the red door and another path appears.

The cues themselves come from the external environment and our internal thoughts, sometimes at the same time. A stimulated cue first activates brands directly *linked* in memory. These direct links arise when the brand and the cue are experienced at the same time (*co-presentation*). Without a direct link to the cue, getting retrieved from memory is extremely unlikely.

For managing brands, this means two things are necessary:

- knowing what cues buyers use when they think of options to buy; and
- building strong, fresh links to these cues.

If your brand's links aren't strong, then a buyer can retrieve other options (usually your competitors' brands). And if one of these options can do the job, then, sorry, that's what usually gets bought. Buyers rarely want more work to go searching for other alternatives if a good enough one is easily available.

Let's work through an example. If you feel *tired*, you might then look for (cue) *something to pick me up*, and so options (soft drink, Pepsi, Starbucks) will then pop into your brain, based on what you have mentally available as a *pick me up*. If one of these options easily works (you know of a Coke vending machine close by), then expending extra energy looking for other alternatives is unnecessary.

If none of the options works (perhaps the vending machine only takes coins and you don't have any cash handy), then you can dredge your memory further for alternatives or ask advice of others. But, in most cases, a quick search of memory can provide more than enough easily buyable options.

A technical, but important, point is that the *direction* (of retrieval) also matters. Just because the brand easily cues something from memory, it doesn't mean that same something can cue the brand just as easily (Holden & Lutz 1992). For example, it is possible that you know that Moroccan-born French brothers started Guess, the clothing brand, but it's unlikely that the cue *French fashion* will ever evoke the brand Guess.

With mental availability we are interested in what cues buyers use when we want our brand to be retrieved (when people are thinking of *something to wear to work*, do they think of Guess?), rather than what people think of when the brand is the cue (what does Guess make them think of?).

Building mental availability

A brand's mental availability is its accessibility from memory across the range of situations and needs that buyers in that category encounter (Romaniuk, 2013). To be bought, a brand must first be thought of—the breadth (how many) and strength (how strong) of the brand's links to relevant cues determine the chance of this happening (Romaniuk & Sharp, 2004).

Cues come from the common experiences that buyers in the category share: for example, we all have birthdays, times we want to treat ourselves, days when we don't have any energy, or experience weather when it is too hot to move. These common thoughts (cues) category buyers use to locate options to buy are useful *category entry points* (CEPs). Attaching the brand to these particular memory structures will increase the chance the brand will come to mind in buying situations. We now expand on these (often neglected) memory structures.

What are category entry points?

Category entry points (CEPs) linkages are pathways to the brand. The more CEPs there are, the more pathways there are, and the more opportunities for the brand to be salient there are. You can think of these CEPs as 'distribution outlets' in the mind (Romaniuk, 2003). When building physical availability, you want your brand to be present in every shopping channel—on the shelf of every supermarket, in every pharmacy, on each retailer website and in every convenience store: CEPs are the cognitive channels that build mental availability.

CEPs represent the buyer's thoughts or influences at the start of buying from the category, pre-brand. They can be purchase situations (at the mall), consumption situations (for a birthday party), the environment the buyer is in (at the beach), who else is present (with the kids), needs (something refreshing) or core benefits that the category can offer (filling snack).

Both internal motivations (for example, feeling hungry) and external situations (for example, to share with the kids) can play a part. Figure 4.2 shows some of the broad questions that can generate a category's CEPs.

Figure 4.2: Framework for CEP generation

CEPs are priority links

Buyers use CEPs to retrieve brands. This makes them attractive associations for the brand. Smart use of advertising accelerates the brand's links to CEPs. A good example of this is McDonald's and breakfast. Would you naturally think of McDonald's at breakfast time if there had not been extensive advertising? Possibly. You might have passed a McDonald's in the morning and noticed it was open, with a smell of hash browns, pancakes and coffee. If you paid enough attention, it might 'click' that McDonald's offers breakfast (though you might easily forget soon after). Then eventually on the way to work one day, when you skipped breakfast at home, you might think, 'I'll pick something up at McDonald's for breakfast today'.

For the many millions of McDonald's buyers, this process would have taken a considerable time to develop—probably much longer than financially desirable for McDonald's. Advertising this CEP in the context of the brand got people through the doors more quickly[2].

As CEPs reflect brand buying or usage experiences, the most common ones can vary across countries. Lifestyles differ because of culture, climate, wealth, religion and infrastructure. Don't assume a one-size-fits-all approach works for CEPs—allow for customisation to the local environment, and allow for evolution over time. While there will be common themes, don't plaster over the differences: these can provide rich insights.

You can determine the relative importance of CEPs by calculating how often each CEP is linked to brands, as the ranking of CEPs from highest to lowest response levels can act as a proxy for relevance[3]. CEPs that are retrieved more often have fresher links to more brands.

The rank order of CEPs across countries can reveal which CEPs are more commonly relevant, and therefore useful in global campaigns—and which can avoid the needless tailoring of messages. CEPs with a higher rank in a particular country or region can then be used in local campaigns as needed.

Psst ... a secret about big brands

The hype about brand differentiation and positioning can easily lead to the conclusion that brands need to be strong on one or two CEPs to be successful. This ignores an important (empirical) fact: *large share brands are linked to a broader range of CEPs than smaller brands*. This breadth of memory structures is a key part of their equity. If you want to create a big brand, you need to link the brand to the many different CEPs in the category—not just one or two.

---

2   Alongside McDonald's altering their physical availability by changing their opening hours as well.

3   This approach of linking frequency with relevance is well established in the typicality and categorisation literature (Rosch & Mervis, 1975), as well as in human memory literature.

For example, let's look at soft drinks in Turkey. The category is dominated by Coca-Cola, but includes local brands such as Cola-Turka, launched in 2003. Its advertising has a deliberate play on Turkish nationalism: for example, showing how American actor Chevy Chase becomes more Turkish after drinking Cola-Turka.

We identified eight soft drink CEPs—such as *on a warm day, something a bit healthy, kids would enjoy it, to treat myself, go well with meals*—and with data from an online survey of soft drink consumers in 2014, calculated how many of these CEPs are linked to each brand (see Figure 4.3). Comparing Coca-Cola and Cola-Turka (which is one-eighth of Coca-Cola's market share), we see that Coca-Cola has *more* people linking it to *more* CEPs than Cola-Turka does. Indeed, 67% of soft drink buyers did not link Cola-Turka to any CEP. Therefore, irrespective of the situation or context of a Turkish soft drink category buyer, Coca-Cola has a much better chance of being thought of than Cola-Turka. For Cola-Turka to grow, it needs to broaden its CEP network in category buyers and be mentally available for more buyers in more buying situations.

Big brands have fresher memory structures for more category buyers across more CEPs—which is the big (mental) difference between big and small brands.

Figure 4.3: Number of CEPs for Coca-Cola and Cola-Turka in Turkey (2014)

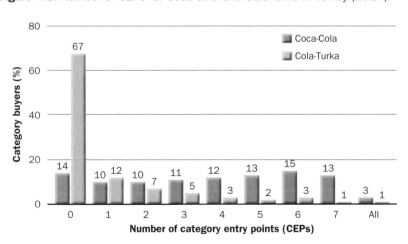

Not one 'consideration set': many context-specific evoked sets

The term *consideration set* refers to the (one) subset of brands that is actively considered for purchase (Howard & Sheth, 1969). Traditional texts refer to a brand establishing itself as part of the consideration set and, even today, many brand-health trackers include a question along the lines of 'which of the following brands would you consider for purchase?'

This idea of a 'one consideration set fits all purchase occasions' is an outdated model, created without modern knowledge about how buyers retain, process and access brand memories. Buyers don't have a single consideration set: this would be a very inefficient use of memory, as at every purchase occasion people would have to retrieve many more, often irrelevant, options than they need.

Table 4.4: Example of how CEPs responses vary across category buyers for soft drinks in Turkey (2014)

CEP	Male, 18–24 years, Bursa	Male, 25–34 years, Istanbul	Female, 18–24 years, other	Female, 25–34 years, Istanbul
Great on a warm day	Coca-Cola Fanta Fruko Uludağ Yedigün	Çamlıca Coca-Cola Pepsi Max Uludağ	Coca-Cola	Akmina Çamlıca Coca-Cola Cola-Turka Esfane Fanta Fruko Frutti
Wake you up	Coca-Cola Pepsi Pepsi Twist	Çamlıca Pepsi Light Pepsi Max Uludağ	Coca-cola	4u Cola Çamlıca Coca-Cola Cola-Turka
Something a bit healthy	Fanta Uludağ	Pepsi Pepsi Max	Schweppes	Akmina Çamlıca Esfane Fruko
Kids would enjoy it	Fanta Uludağ Yedigün	Fanta Coca-Cola	Fruko	Coca-Cola Fruko
When I want to treat myself	Coca-Cola Fanta Yedigün	Pepsi	None	Akmina Çamlıca Fanta Fruko

Table 4.4 shows the variation across buyers and CEPs for four soft drink buyers in Turkey. Brands vary, the number of brands also varies, and the sets are mixes of local brands such as Uludağ and Yedigün as well as global brands such as Coca-Cola, Pepsi and Fanta.

Remember it's not just about internal needs—external factors also shape what buyers retrieve. In the morning, coffee brands might be more salient as options to *pick me up*, while in the afternoon on a hot day, its more likely to be cold beverages. This contextual influence on retrieval also largely happens without conscious thought, and creates a range of (more efficient) sets that contain brands relevant to the immediate situation.

In other words, there is not one consideration set but many context-specific evoked sets, which means there is no real benefit in asking people directly what brands they consider. The answer will always be: it depends …

Table 4.4 again illustrates the advantage held by large brands, with Coca-Cola being present in 10 out of 16 cells (4 buyers x 4 CEPs), while much smaller Cola-Turka is only in two. Big brands are mentally available for more people in more buying situations.

Categories often have a range of CEPs and a cornucopia of brands that consumers can think of for each[4]. Measuring mental availability via a single cue or a single response to a cue is therefore misguided. To gauge a brand's mental availability, you need to look across multiple CEPs to gain a good representation of the brand's competitiveness.

Mental availability metrics

The more links to CEPs a brand has, relative to competitors, the greater the chance is that it will be salient in any buying situation. To reflect this, Romaniuk (2013) draws on a representative set of CEPs across key brands to calculate a *mental market share*. This approach focuses on

---

4   The one possible exception is very light category buyers who typically only know about and buy the largest brand in the category (the natural monopoly law discussed in Chapter 2). These buyers might only think of one brand for any CEP they encounter.

the brand's performance across the whole CEP network rather than the brand's performance on any specific CEP[5].

The following are some key metrics to assess the strength of the brand's memory structures:

- *mental market share*—the brand's percentage of CEP associations, of the total CEP associations for the brand and competitors. It reflects the brand's relative retrieval competitiveness in the whole category.
- *mental penetration*—the percentage of category buyers who link the brand with at least one CEP. This measures brand awareness more in line with associative network theories of memory, as it calculates the possibility of retrieval across the multiple potential pathways to retrieve the brand. The higher the mental penetration, the more category buyers have the brand mentally available.
- *network size*—how many CEPs the brand is linked to in the minds of those aware: the wider the network, the more potential pathways for brand retrieval. This metric is useful for assessing if advertising is maintaining or building the CEP network.

While these metrics often correlate with their sales equivalents at a single point in time—this is normal for brand-health metrics; disparities between mental and sales market share can highlight issues with distribution, marketing mix (for example, is the price too high?) or messaging (for example, has our message been too narrow?)[6].

Importantly, these metrics can help track the performance of marketing activity in building long-term memory structures, particularly

---

5   See Romaniuk and Sharp (2000) for a method for determining a brand's performance on any one specific CEP for brand image analysis.
6   Romaniuk (2013) shows how the NBD Dirichlet model identifies deviations in the absence of sales data or in categories such as services where repeat buying data is not easily available.

amongst light and non-buyers of the brand (from whom growth will come). For example, a campaign highlighting a new CEP should grow network size; a media schedule that has wider reach should build mental penetration; and a better correct branding score for a campaign should build both metrics.

Table 4.5 is an example of these metrics for phone handsets in India. We identified CEPs to cover a wide range of aspects of mobile phone handsets including pricing, size, durability and after-sales service: for example, *easy to use*, *battery would last a long time*, *offers a design I would be proud to show others*, *works well for online shopping*, or *would be good for social media*.

The metrics show again how category buyers know more of the larger brands, for more CEPS. For example, Samsung is accessible for 90% of category buyers, for 10.8 CEPs (out of 16). In contrast, HTC is accessible for 53% of buyers, for 6.8 CEPs. We can also see some exceptions: for example, Micromax has a higher mental penetration and lower network size for its rank order. This suggests the brand has spent too long on a single message, and needs to broaden its links to CEPs to make it fresh in a wider range of phone-buying situations.

The correlation between mental market share and market share (value) (figures from Press Trust of India, 2013) for a subset of brands in the Indian market is shown in Figure 4.4. We can see the brands generally in the same rank order, with a notable exception being Apple iPhones—which have higher mental market share than sales. This disparity is likely due to its higher price creating a barrier to purchase. In contrast Lava and Karbonn, which are cheaper local brands, have lower mental availability than their sales would suggest. These brands might not be as mentally available, but find buyers in-store due to their low price.

Table 4.5: Example of mental availability metrics for phone handsets in India (2014)

Brand	Mental market share (%)	Mental penetration (%)	Network size (mean)
Samsung	21	90	10.8
Nokia	17	85	9.3
Apple iPhone	15	80	8.3
Micromax	9	69	5.8
HTC	8	53	6.8
BlackBerry	7	60	5.6
LG	5	48	4.5
Motorola	4	44	4.1
Karbonn	4	54	3.1
Lava	3	45	2.7
XOLO	2	33	3.4
Videocon	2	38	2.2
Huawei	2	32	2.4
Celkon	2	37	2.1

Figure 4.4: Comparison between mental market share and market share (value sales) for phone handset market in India (where data was available)

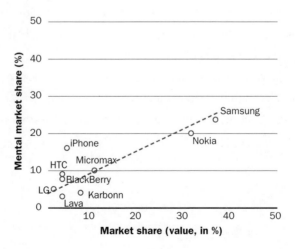

Building fresh brand memories

Mental availability is an ongoing battle for memory freshness. As time moves on from each encounter with a brand, buyer memories fade. Seeing competitors' brands also make the brand's memories harder to retrieve. Remember that many of your brand's customers also buy your competitors (Chapter 3), and so will notice their advertising. This is why the reach and continuity of marketing activities are important (more on this in Chapter 6).

If the branding is noticeable and the messages relevant, advertising can help category buyers maintain and build mental availability. Even the biggest brands have many buyers with very few fresh, accessible brand associations. For example, if we examine the CEP distribution across Coca-Cola and Jarritos (a local soft drink with cola and fruit variants) in Mexico we find 70% of Jarritos buyers (the smaller brand) have five or fewer CEP linkages, compared to 35% of Coca-Cola buyers have five or fewer CEP linkages (see Figure 4.5). With many current buyers holding few CEPs about the brand, refreshing their few accessible CEPs is important just to maintain market share. To grow, you need to build freshness across category buyers *and* CEPs.

Figure 4.5: Distribution of CEPs for Coca-Cola and Jarritos in Mexico (2014)

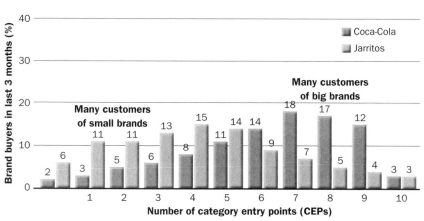

Brand positioning = your advertised messages

It's time to reposition brand positioning.

Traditional texts tell us that a strong brand equals a strongly positioned brand. We have shown this to be misguided—strong brands don't rely on a single proposition but are mentally available across wide range of category needs.

A brand's position is seldom mysterious—your marketing efforts create it, particularly advertising because of its potential for wide reach[7]. The strength of any position is a function of how well these messages have cut through and become linked to the brand in buyer memory, particularly amongst the brand's very light or non-buyers.

When well-branded advertising builds memory structures, the brand gets a higher than expected response on that attribute. But competitor interference and the fading of memories over time mean that this heightened response is a temporary rather than permanent state—if the reinforcement ceases (through a change of message or poor quality in creativity), this 'excess response' reverts to normal (Romaniuk & Nicholls, 2006; Romaniuk & Sharp 2000).

A valuable test of the effectiveness of advertised messages is to see the brand is better known for a specific attribute than it should be for its size. But, over time, the attributes the brand is well known for should change as the advertised message changes.

It is also important to separate out execution objectives from that of a total campaign, as these often confuse those who fear a multi-message approach to advertising. A single execution needs a single clear message but building mental availability requires spotlighting different parts of the broader CEP network in different executions.

---

7   Unless it is a functional quality of the brand that non-users can infer from the name such as Royal Bank of Scotland and 'Scottish'.

When designing a message strategy—ask the following questions:

- which CEP will exposure to this execution build? Will this be obvious, even for the lightest category and brand buyer[8]?
- is this CEP often useful for a large number of people? The more common the CEP, the more impact the advertising can have. The more obscure the CEP, the fewer choice situations the advertising can affect.
- when was the last time you promoted this CEP? If it featured in a recent campaign, perhaps see if other CEPs have been neglected, as freshening these memories might benefit the brand more.

Use the measurement of the brand's 'position' to test whether your advertising has been successful in building links to that CEP. But don't expect (or want) to hold onto that position forever. If your advertising is working, as the message changes, so too should what the brand is known for. This change in position reflects the success of the newer campaign.

What about country of origin?

The importance of *country of origin* (COO) sparks a continuing debate. Is it a benefit (as in the case of German cars) or a drawback (as in the case of Guatemalan sparkling wine)? The general evidence is that effects are localised. For some countries, in some categories, for some brands an effect (either positive or negative) is possible. COO usually plays on cultural stereotypes, and is different from the idea of provenance—which is where (typically) agricultural products draw on a link to the source region or a protected process, such as in the case of Parma ham or feta cheese. Provenance can be an important brand memory, but it does require the buyer to be educated as to its benefits, which will interest only a small percentage of category buyers.

---

8   Note: This test should be applied to all marketing activities, not just advertising.

COO does not need to be real—it can be simply signalled in the brand name, packaging, characters and taglines. Crabtree & Evelyn looks very English, doesn't it? The company was in fact founded in 1972 in the USA; in 1996 it was sold to a Malaysian corporation and in 2012 a Hong Kong investment company bought it. Buyers are educated by marketing, and so change their perceptions of the value of an origin to a brand or product. For example, Chilean wine was unheard of twenty years ago, and generally considered poor quality. A decade later you can see Chilean wine on restaurant menus commanding decent prices. Perceptions of COO, like most opinions, can change with exposure and experience.

If you are in a category where historical COO memories *could* be evoked, these are the important questions to ask:

- is COO likely to be incorporated into a CEP that category buyers use to think of brands? For example, a buyer might decide he or she wants a Spanish wine to take to dinner when a friend is cooking paella, and any brand without a history of signalling its 'Spanishness' is unlikely to be mentally available. In which case, COO can be a useful memory to build, provided it is a credible claim to make (and your category buyers eat lots of paella!).
- might COO be used to reject a brand? In which case references, to COO should be minimised.

In today's global world, different countries are emerging as powerhouses in a wide range of industries (witness South Korea's growth in electronics, China's in phone handsets). The spread of manufacturing facilities also means that origin itself is difficult to pin down (most people think of Apple products as from the USA, even though they are largely manufactured in China). These changes to the economic and production landscape mean that COO will not be of major concern to most brands in most categories in most countries.

Use COO if it can help build mental availability; ignore or downplay it if it could lead to brand rejection—just like any other mental structure.

Love, hate and the wide chasm between them

Over many decades, the idea of emotional attachments has been dressed up with different names. More recently it is called 'brand love' but let's not get fooled by old concepts with new labels; previous incarnations such as brand attitude, brand relationships and brand engagement all touted the same idea.

People can develop feelings about brands. It's just that these feelings are typically weak (it's fine/okay/does the job) and reflect, rather than predict, their own buying behaviour (I buy it so therefore I like it). We should be wary of giving these feelings too much weight in the buying process, simply because very little evidence supports any disproportionate attention, including for emerging markets and high-involvement categories.

Two common mistakes inflate the importance of strong emotions about brands.

Mistake 1: Assuming non-buying equals brand rejection

One mistaken assumption is that most non-brand users have actively rejected the brand. Testing by the Ehrenberg–Bass Institute across more than 500 brands in 24 product categories and 23 countries reveals that explicit brand rejection is low, even in emerging markets (see Figure 4.6). For the vast majority of brands, lack of mental availability is a far more important battle than overcoming buyer rejection.

Mistake 2: Assuming everyone has a defined attitude

It is easy to inflate the importance of attitudes to brands by forcing people to create an on-the-spot opinion, with limited response options. For example, in the absence of a 'don't know' or 'no opinion' option on a scale, non-users usually default to the mid-point response (say 4 out of 7, or 3 out of 5). This assigns quite a larger value to no response, particularly for small brands that will tend to have more non-users without an opinion,

Figure 4.6: Rejection levels in different markets (taken from Romaniuk, Nenycz-Thiel & Truong, 2011)

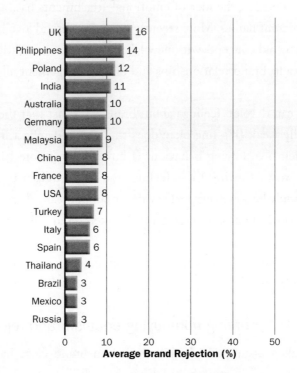

and gives the impression of a stronger attitude than is really present (Romaniuk 2008).

Having a full spectrum of attitudes in the response set, including no attitude at all, will give you a more realistic picture of the strength and dispersion of attitudes to the brand. A non-response is sometimes just that—don't know/don't think about it/don't care!

All you need is love?

One extreme emotion that has captured the attention (passion?) of marketers is brand love ('the strongest emotion of all' says advertising guru Kevin Roberts, 2004). It is suggested that building brand love will lead to brand growth but the weight of evidence does not support these claims. Other forays into the importance of emotional attachment to the brand, such as *Lovemarks* (Roberts, 2004) or engagement with the brand on social media, have highlighted that these extreme feelings are rare, and of little consequence to a brand's market share.

Big brands generate more positive attitudes than small brands but there is scant evidence to suggest these (stronger) positive attitudes drive usage. A more typical attitude profile is a few people loving the brand, a few people hating the brand, and the vast majority thinking it is a perfectly okay brand to buy.

How Brands Grow discussed the foolishness of worrying about deep feelings about brands: we won't give any more oxygen to this distraction except to say we see them equally irrelevant in emerging markets and others such as new, high-involvement, infrequently bought categories. Many buyers in these markets and categories are inexperienced but this does not make them besotted fools for brands.

Conclusion

Building mental availability requires attaching the brand to memory structures that are useful for buyers when they are thinking about buying. In this chapter we introduced CEPs—the cues buyers use to think of options to buy—which are crucial to understand. CEPs underpin mental availability: the wider and fresher the network of CEPs, the more likely the brand will be salient in buying situations. These are, therefore, important memory structures for a brand to build.

Unfortunately most brand-health trackers tend to under-represent CEPs; this is a missed opportunity. Directing efforts to understand and monitor a brand's performance on relevant CEPs helps ensure that the tracker is capturing mental availability as well as positioning.

As CEPs are about the content of memory, rather than the structure, it is important to ensure that you have the list of priority CEPs for each of your markets. With these lists you can identify opportunities for messaging in global and local campaigns.

The outdated ideas of consideration set and positioning can be made relevant to current knowledge about buyer memory and behaviour. But, instead of one consideration set, we now refer to many different context-specific evoked sets. And instead of narrowcasting a brand to be strongly positioned, we now think of positioning as a transient reflection of the successful processing of current advertised messages.

5

Leveraging Distinctive Assets

Jenni Romaniuk

Distinctive assets are non-brand name elements, such as colours, logos, characters and fonts that can trigger the brand for category buyers. This chapter shows you how to choose your distinctive assets wisely, and how to execute them (well), both in advertising and on pack to build both mental and physical availability.

We also discuss identity strategies for launching variants, as well as the role of meaning and the brand's position in selecting distinctive assets.

Meet our owl

This chapter is about identifying, selecting and developing distinctive assets, and avoiding common traps, particularly for big, established brands.

To kick off this conversation, I'd like to introduce you to the Ehrenberg–Bass Institute's owl[1]. You will see her throughout the book. Our corporate sponsors might also recognise her from corporate reports, and email updates. She gives the Ehrenberg–Bass Institute brand name a visually rich image that signals and reminds you about the brand in different contexts, such as in the middle of a page, where a big 'Ehrenberg–Bass Institute' would distract from the text! This chapter is about her, and other brand assets that perform a similar task.

What's in a (brand) name?

Every brand has a name that distinguishes it from other brands. This name anchors the brand in the memory of category buyers, and attracts other memory structures that populate the overall picture of what the brand is and what it can do.

In addition to the brand name, other memory structures come to represent the brand in buyer memory. These representatives, or distinctive assets, are the colours, logos, sounds, characters, slogans and the like that can trigger the brand for category buyers. These distinctive assets often represent the brand in non-word form, which can be advantageous for the brain's attention to, and processing of, the brand.

The brand, in the form of a name (word), taps into our semantic memory but (remember from Chapter 4) this is only a small part of our complex memory. Faces, shapes, colours, and sounds all activate different neurological processes. Representing the brand in different forms takes advantage of the many different processes human brains can undertake.

---

1   Suggestions for a name are welcome!

This diversity of brand identity increases the quantity *and* quality of a brand's presence in its environment.

The many types of distinctive assets

The opportunity (and curse) of distinctive assets is the many types of assets to choose from (see Figure 5.1). A history of testing distinctive assets in many categories and countries has taught us that anything can be a strong distinctive asset—you just need to choose wisely and execute well. This chapter provides guidelines to help you do both.

Figure 5.1: Types of distinctive assets

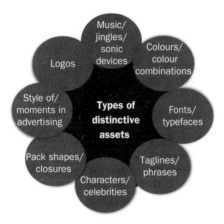

Distinctiveness is not differentiation

Before we get too deeply into the topic of distinctive assets, it is important to reiterate some points from *How Brands Grow* about the relationship between distinctiveness and differentiation.

Differentiation is put forward as a meaningful difference that leads to purchase—its roots are in classic economic theory. So if your car offers all-wheel drive when no other car does, and (at least some) buyers value all-wheel drive, then these buyers (should) flock to your brand because it has something other brands do not.

Distinctiveness is the brand's identity and how it is recognised (over competitors) and includes any sensory element that triggers the brand (visual, auditory, smell, touch). Distinctiveness is not why you buy something but how you know which brand it is, or how to find the brand. For example, you don't buy Red Bull because you particularly want a drink with blue and silver pattern on it, *but* the blue and silver pattern on the can is one of the ways you know you are reaching for a Red Bull and not, say, Monster energy drink.

These are very separate concepts—one is not a subset or a replacement for the other. Mixing them up is simply sloppy thinking.

Step 1: Choosing wisely

Consider the practicalities

With many types of distinctive assets to choose from, first take into account a practical consideration: what is your likely media mix? The media mix will determine the value of video, audio, static picture or text-type assets. An obvious example is that an audio asset is extremely helpful if radio is a key medium.

Consider the brand's history

Can anything in the brand's past be resurrected? Brands with a long history have also usually had a number of different brand managers, each eager to put their own stamp on the brand's identity. Looking through past iterations of creative advertising and packaging can uncover distinctive assets that are known to category buyers and therefore possible to reactivate. It is much easier to refresh an existing memory than to develop a new one, so harnessing history can be a way of quickly creating a strong identity.

Is the brand's identity overweight in one type of asset? What have you been investing in? If you have been switching between two or three taglines, this review of the current identity creates an opportunity to rationalise and focus on building up one to become a strong distinctive asset.

Obtain some numbers to inform your choices

Next find evidence about the strength of current assets to work out their potential for use or development. The Ehrenberg–Bass Institute has developed an approach (Romaniuk & Nenycz-Thiel, 2014) with two metrics to quantify the strength and potential of any distinctive asset:

- *fame*—how many category buyers link the brand name to the element
- *uniqueness*—the share of responses for that asset that goes to brand (versus competitors' brands).

The metrics capture the likelihood that the asset will trigger the brand name amongst category buyers. The results help you prioritise which assets to build, and provide a benchmark for measuring the impact of distinctive asset–building activities.

Low levels of fame mean that the asset is not (yet) valuable, especially if the brand has substantial market share. It could still be a candidate for investment, particularly if it adds neurological richness by hitting a sense or part of the brain that other assets don't.

If competitors are also linked to the element, this will be reflected in low uniqueness, which should be of concern. This metric is independent of brand size, which means small market share brands can score as highly as big brands. Low uniqueness suggests that investment in this asset will struggle to gain return, with a high risk of the misattribution to other brands. Trying to reclaim this ground is risky and requires extremely strong direct reference to the brand name to minimise the triggering of competitors' brands.

Plotting the position of the asset on the Distinctive Asset Grid (Figure 5.2) on the four quadrants indicates its potential. The cut off is at the 50% level as this represents the two tipping points in the brand's favour. If an asset has 50% or more fame, then category buyers are more likely than not to trigger the brand; if an asset has 50% or more uniqueness, then it is the dominant brand retrieved. The ideal point is 100% fame and

100% uniqueness. Don't be distracted by industry norms or averages; the objective for any distinctive asset should be uniqueness of 100% *and* fame of 100%.

Figure 5.2: Distinctive Asset Grid[2] (developed by Jenni Romaniuk)

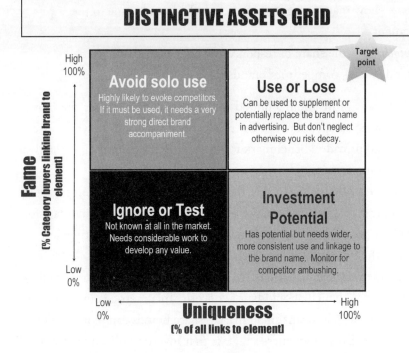

The quadrants reveal the relative strategic potential and challenges, if marketers want to use or develop a specific asset.

• *Usable* (over 50% fame *and* uniqueness)—this quadrant is called 'Use or Lose' as it identifies the strongest distinctive assets and reminds us that without reinforcement, the assets are likely to be lost. These assets still need to be executed prominently to keep buyers' memory structures fresh.

---

2   If you would like to use this grid, please be in contact and I can send you a colour copy.

- *Investable* (over 50% uniqueness but less than 50% fame)—this is the next most interesting quadrant as it reflects assets with potential. The brand is recognised as being unique, but is not well known for the asset. Broadening how many people link the brand to the asset can shift the asset to Usable status.
- *Avoid solo use* (over 50% fame but less than 50% uniqueness)—this is a tricky quadrant as the asset has fame, but is linked to multiple brands. This is typical of assets that are (or are becoming) generic category, and usually due to new entrants mirroring the cues of the established brands. It is hard to give up an asset when fame is high but use it without strong direct branding risks giving valuable mental real estate to competitors' brands.
- *Ignore or Test* (less than 50% fame *and* uniqueness)—these elements have nothing that gives them a head start over others. The elements could be new to the brand; lack cut through; or are much stronger for competitors. Delving more deeply into past efforts and current competitive links can help reveal which of these is the case.

Distinctiveness measurement in action

To illustrate the potential that brand assets can have, and how this can vary across countries, we tested the strength of assets from well-known brands in four countries (the USA, China, Brazil and South Africa). The assets and brands tested included the following:

- logos from car brands such as BMW, Volkswagen, Hyundai and Chevrolet
- fonts from Google and IBM
- logos from sports wear brands such Nike, Puma and Adidas
- images and logos from soft drink brands such as Coca-Cola, Pepsi and Red Bull
- logos from fast food brands such as KFC and Domino's

- Ronald McDonald from McDonald's
- logos from two global aid brands, Red Cross and Unicef.

For each country, we calculated each asset's fame and uniqueness metrics[3], to see the variation across assets and countries. Here are highlights of the results.

- In fast food, Domino's and Burger King have a usable asset in the USA but only investable assets in other countries—with very low fame in China. In contrast, Ronald McDonald (character) is a stronger asset, usable in three countries and borderline investable– usable in China. The KFC logo is also highly usable in three countries, but drops to investable level in Brazil.
- Four of the car logos (BMW, Volkswagen, Hyundai and Chevrolet) are usable in all countries. Reflecting its marketing investment, Hyundai is stronger in emerging markets than in the USA.
- Apple has the strongest overall performance for technology brands, with fame scores of 90% or higher and uniqueness over 99% in all four countries. Google's font is usable in three countries, and investable in China, while IBM's font is investable in all countries. In contrast the HTC logo is in the ignore quadrant in all four countries.
- Of the sportswear brands, unsurprisingly, the Nike swoosh is strong in all four countries but it has strong competition. Logos from Adidas and Puma also achieve usable status in all four countries, although not quite at Nike's level. Results are mixed for ASICs and Reebok logos, with most scores in the investable quadrant.
- In the battle of the soft drinks logos, we found Pepsi and Red Bull at usable level in all four countries, with Red Bull strong in China,

---

3   Samples of n = 300 online survey in each country, conducted March 2015.

but eclipsed by Pepsi in other countries. Coca-Cola's red-and-white wave image is usable in three countries, but only investable in China. This might be due to Coca-Cola's lack of emphasis on the colour red in recent times, with the launch of Coke Zero (black) and Coca-Cola Life (green).

- Finally the two non-profit brands Red Cross and Unicef provide a contrast of results from this sector. Red Cross is usable in all countries, while Unicef is only investable in three. The mother and child image in the Unicef logo is confused with other women and children's charities.

Figures 5.3, 5.4, 5.5 and 5.6 show the grids for each country, although, due to crowding in each chart, sometimes only a selection of assets tested is shown.

Figure 5.3: Distinctive asset results for key brand assets in the USA (2015)

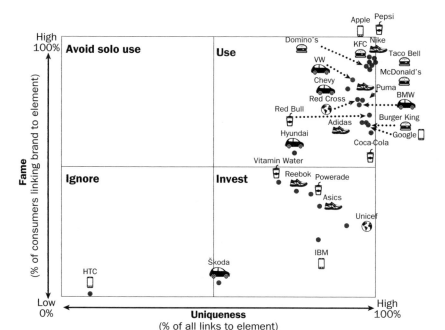

Figure 5.4: Distinctive asset results for key brand assets in China (2015)

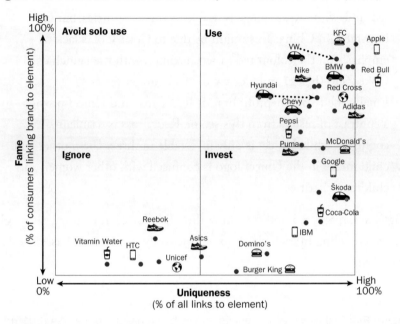

Figure 5.5: Distinctive asset results for key brand assets in South Africa (2015)

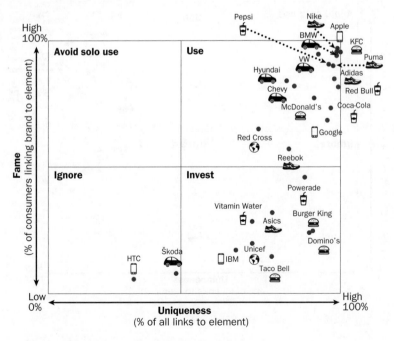

Figure 5.6: Distinctive asset results for key brand assets in Brazil (2015)

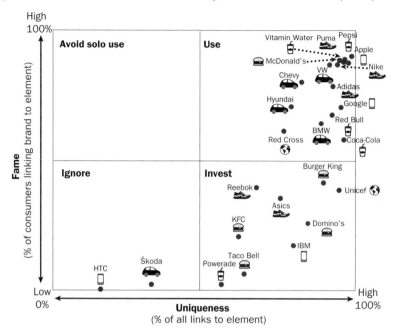

Step 2: How to execute well

A common question is how long it takes to build up a distinctive asset to usable status. The answer depends on how well you implement the following three steps:

Step 2A: Reach all category buyers. Only those buyers exposed to the brand with the distinctive asset can build memory linkages. If your advertising reaches 50% of category buyers, then 50% have a chance of learning that the asset is linked to the brand. Put simply, a reach of 50% builds distinctive assets quicker than a reach of 30%, but not as quickly as if you reach 80% of category buyers.

Step 2B: Create prominent co-presentation moments. To establish or strengthen the link between the brand name and the asset, category buyers need moments where the two are together and these moments need to be a noticeable part of all communications. The more prominent these moments are, the quicker you will establish distinctive assets amongst those who are exposed.

Step 2C: Consistency. Every exposure is a 'do or decay' branding moment. The window to insert the brand into people's lives is small and short-lived. Consistency is key to making every exposure count.

Inconsistency is more than just a missed opportunity to strengthen a distinctive asset; it sets the brand's identity backwards by creating associations that interfere with future retrieval. This is a mistake often made when creating a brand identity for variants.

TAKE THE TEST

A useful exercise is to lay out, on one big table, all of the brand collateral that a category buyer is likely to see. Don't just confine it to printed material; print out web pages, presence in online stores, any variants that draw on the brand name—indeed, anything that the category buyer might see.

What jumps out at you as you look across the table? Is it a sea of red? Or any other colour? Does a character continually jump out? An expression?

Do all of the items look like they have come from the same family? Or do a few oddities look like they belong somewhere else?

This is the first step to check your execution and eliminate inconsistencies.

Make smart branding choices for variants and extensions

A new variant or extension comes with a new design. The design priority is typically to separate the new launch from the parent brand so one can be easily distinguished from the other. But this misses the big challenge: *both* options are fighting to be found in the cluttered shopping environment. Having a very different-looking variant might make it easier to find the variant when next to the parent, but there are drawbacks:

- it misses an opportunity to help the brand portfolio stand out from clutter by fragmenting the identity across packs that are on shelf

- it creates less certainty around the assets of the parent brand, thereby weakening the parent brand's identity.

When launching a variant/extension think parent brand first, variant second. Variants come and go but the parent brand should be a constant priority. Variant lines need to retain consistency with the parent brand, particularly in emerging markets with many little or nano retailers who are unlikely to stock the full range of any brand. The brand portfolio needs to be easy to identify, irrespective of the variants stocked.

Design for the variant in two stages. Whether you are designing packaging, a website, online or print promotions doesn't matter: whatever is being designed, these two steps are vital:

- First, incorporate the umbrella distinctive assets—these establish the parent–variant brand link and keep building distinctive assets for the parent brand.
- Then add on the variant specific assets, which might be twists on the parent assets, such as using a different shade of the colour, or a pattern. For example, if dark blue is a parent brand asset, then perhaps make the variant packaging stripes in dark blue and another colour to keep a key colour consistent, but still generate a distinct visual image. If a key asset is a character, perhaps create a family relation that can be the voice for the variant but still retain the link to the parent.

This two-step approach will avoid diluting the distinctive assets of the parent brand, but still help category buyers find the variant.

Don't get caught up in the meaning of it all

Marketing and advertising have great storytellers, and it is easy to get caught up in the mythology and romanticism of it all. But buyers rarely know (or care) about this rich allegory. For example, when you see Johnnie Walker's striding man, do you realise that he was recently reversed from walking left to walking right to be seen as moving forward and progressing toward fulfilling his personal goals (Epstein, 2014)?

When we are selecting distinctive assets, a common distraction is to try to use the brand's mission or value or purpose or *raison d'être*. This short-term strategy can backfire in the long term as the brand evolves. Think about some of the biggest brands today and how they have evolved in terms of their product mix: remember Apple used to be a computer company, Starbucks was all about coffee, McDonald's talked only about hamburgers and Amazon once just sold books. Having a distinctive asset closely linked to what the company offers or stands for *now* means potentially modifying or abandoning it in the future, diminishing the value of past distinctive asset–building activities.

In the context of the category, the brand name should be the strongest meaning for any distinctive asset. Be concerned about other meanings only if they are holding back that key linkage to the brand. This includes your current positioning strategy.

Treat brand identity and positioning like oil and water

It is tempting to draw from the deep well of positioning for potential distinctive assets. In an effort to kill two birds with one stone, advertisers try to mix together identity and messaging and have moments in the advertising stand for both the brand's position and the brand name. This is short-sighted.

If we remember back to Chapter 4, positioning is best 'positioned' as a direct outcome of effective communication of advertising messages. To build mental availability you need breadth *and* freshness of category entry points (CEPs). If your distinctive asset is linked to the current execution's message or CEP, will it still work when the brand's message changes to highlight another CEP? Or will you have to abandon that distinctive asset?

The smartest long-term strategy is to create a brand identity that is independent of the brand's current advertising messages and positioning. This gives you the freedom to adapt the brand's message over campaigns but keep the brand's identity consistent and keep freshening these links in memory. Remember, 'use or lose': even the strongest distinctive asset will decay in buyers' memories if not used.

Advertise messages for the short term but build a brand identity for the long term. Mixing the two makes it more difficult to achieve either.

Distinctive assets and mental availability

Mental availability is the propensity of the brand to be salient in buying situations. To build mental availability, a brand needs to have fresh links to a wide range of CEPs. Category buyers build to links to CEPs when they are exposed to the brand alongside the CEP. Distinctive assets help the branding side of the equation to build mental availability (having a relevant message is the other side). Remember: the easier it is to process the brand, the more attention a viewer can give to the message.

Different touch-points help us insert our brand into a buyer's life, and freshen the brand's memory structures: *if the brand is a noticeable part of the advertising*. Distinctive assets can help the brand gain attention in the following ways.

- *Increase the amount of branding within an advertisement*
  Distinctive assets provide additional branding devices.
  Advertisers (often misguidedly) fear boring buyers if too much of the advertisement's real estate is devoted to the brand name. The brand name is therefore typically a small part of any advertisement, with more time and space spent on creative and messaging elements (Romaniuk, 2009). Branding via distinctive assets can mitigate this fear, and increase branding content (Hartnett, 2011).
- *Broaden the audience for the brand exposure*
  People with low literacy can use shapes, colours or characters as brand identifiers. This allows the branding to reach more category buyers. This is particularly important in emerging markets, where education levels vary considerably, including amongst owners of traditional small and nano retail outlets. But even in developed markets, literacy is an issue, with 14% of the US population unable to read and 21% reading below a fifth-grade level (Huffington Post, 2013).

- *Provide script-independent branding*
  Written language in countries such as China, Thailand, Greece and Russia use different scripts for letters. Representing the brand in non-word forms, such as logos or characters, can create consistency across language types. This is useful for campaigns that span multiple countries.

- *Improve the quality of brand execution*
  Branding execution is not just about the quantity of branding—quality also matters (Romaniuk, 2009). Distinctive assets improve the quality of brand execution by paving the way for smarter execution tactics that often face resistance when directly involving the brand name. For example, early brand exposure in television advertising is a proven tactic to increase correct branding, but advertisers often worry that buyers will switch off once they see the brand name and miss the rest of the advertisement. Drawing on a distinctive asset can overcome this resistance to early branding[4].

- *Increase the neuro-richness of the brand*
  Within an execution, distinctive assets can, therefore, help the brand in forms that tap into a wider variety of memory processes, activating more of the brain. Using distinctive assets can help the brand compete for viewer attention in the face of competition from sexier aspects of the creative execution.

- *Connect executions across media platforms*
  Operating in today's media environment requires a flexible approach to media choices. To reach a large, diverse, potential buyer population, campaigns might need to stretch from sophisticated digital technology to catch the young to more traditional radio to reach commuters to posters on neighbourhood streets to reach homemakers on their way to do the household

---

4   The use of effective brand execution, rather than just adding more branding, becomes even more important as video advertising is getting shorter, with five second ads and six second videos gaining popularity—these mean less time for every thing, including branding.

shopping. Distinctive assets connect executions across media in a multi-platform campaign, providing a linchpin that still allows for variation in creative elements to maximise the strengths of different media formats.

- *Connect past campaigns with the current executions*
  When launching a new campaign, everyone's attention is on the new: new message, new look and feel, new talent, and new media (understandably—it's exciting!). But we need to also be confident that category buyers who see the new campaign know which brand it is for. Distinctive assets provide a brand-consistent look and feel to any execution, so the buyer files it away quickly and correctly. Current campaigns can then capitalise on past campaigns, rather than the viewer needing to start afresh each time.

Distinctive assets and physical availability

Most retail environments are rife with competitive clutter. A mentally available brand might not be bought if another option is easier to find. Buyers are distracted; anything that is hard to find is likely to stay lost. Distinctive assets help the brand's *prominence* in its retail environment, making it easy to find.

Distinctive assets can be displayed on packs, in promotional material and as part of in-store advertising. Packaging distinctive assets are particularly important in retailing environments because competitors are usually in the same visual field. Packs also go home with buyers and can reinforce these assets between buying occasions. Visual assets that involve the pack, and that can be used on shelf and online, are particularly valuable to cultivate.

The importance of packaging distinctive assets

Packaging is one of the most common touch-points seen, particularly in emerging markets (see Chapter 6). Packs appear in advertising but it is on shelf where they can make or break a sale. As products are often side by side with competing ones, packaging needs to 'pop' in the retail environment. Distinctive assets give a focal point for search (such as looking for the purple one or the one with the red top) or provide a hook to catch the eye of the buyer scanning the shelf. These assets also provide a way of describing the brand, to ourselves and to others. In emerging markets, shoppers often buy from small local stores where they ask shopkeepers for the brand. Strong visual assets means buyers can describe the brand and shopkeepers can find the brand more easily.

Packaging change, under the guise of updating, is a common tactical error. Changing the pack is practically never buyer friendly[5], as the diversion from learned assets means the buyer has to work harder to find the brand.

Showing visual distinctive assets both in advertising and on-shelf can bridge out-of-store and in-store activities. Here is a question for you to think about: which distinctive assets do buyers use to find your brand? Is it the colour? The shape? The logo? Or another image on the pack? Do you have evidence to support your answer? Remember: it is not just about how your brand's pack differs from others—it is how visible and well known this difference is to buyers. As parents tend to overestimate their children's capabilities, brand managers tend to be overly optimistic about the number and strength of their brand's distinctive assets. Without objective metrics, you risk only finding out which distinctive assets are important for your competitiveness in retail environments the Tropicana way (which is when you change something and sales drop).

Simply having a colour or logo on the pack does not automatically make it a distinctive asset; competitors and other facets of the environment also matter. For example, we find colour to be important for standing out on shelf (Gaillard, Sharp & Romaniuk, 2006). But, with a limited range of primary colours and the tendency for categories to flock to the

---

5   The only packaging change we know of that is likely to be buyer friendly is a change to bring a distinctive asset onto the pack or make it more prominent by removing distracting material that consumers don't use to identify the brand. Such changes make it easier for the buyer to find the brand, such as Tropicana bringing back the straw and orange onto its pack.

similar (such as yellow for butter, red for tomato pasta sauce and purple for lavender-scented variants), colour is also a very competitive type of distinctive asset. This makes unique ownership of any colour difficult to establish without careful selection and execution (Major, Tanaka & Romaniuk, 2014).

Smart execution of colour can help minimise the risk of competitor sameness. Don't just think which colour; think of how you might use that colour as part of an integrated design. A good example of this is HSBC's advertising, which consistently uses a thick red border. The colour red is relatively common in banking, so executing this colour as a border creates a unique, easily identifiable advertising style.

Distinctive assets and the digital world

Clutter thy name is web page! When designing the brand's visual identity to stand out, think about all competitive environments, including online. Even if your brand is on the first page for shoppers, competitor clutter is rife. In most online shops, the pack or the logo makes up the brand's largest real estate on any page. Any individual brand's real estate is usually quite small—which makes it hard to see intricate details such as cursive fonts or detailed images. Visual assets that can be seen, even when the pack or logo is small, are very valuable in this environment.

Ehrenberg–Bass Institute research by Major (2014) shows that branding via distinctive assets helps an online advertisement gain greater cut-through than the same advertisement with the brand name only. He also found that visual images are also more effective than taglines, similar to that found in print advertising (Hartnett, 2011).

Visual distinctive assets, with features such as colours and shapes, are visually richer than the brand name as a word, but it is more than just the visuals that draw attention: it is the link to the brand name that makes it feel familiar. An analogy is when you enter a crowded room: you might be more likely to notice someone who is very attractive, but you are also drawn to notice the people you know, irrespective of how attractive they are!

The optimal branding design for online advertising, to obtain viewer attention, is a visually rich image *and* that image having a strong, unique linkage to the brand name.

Figure 5.7: The equation for optimal online branding design

Compiling a distinctive asset palette

The broad strategic aim of a distinctive asset palette is to have a set of distinctive assets that can be used across media, in different ways to create a consistent, neurologically rich set of branding options.

Therefore, when you are designing a distinctive assets palette, think diversity. A diverse palette of distinctive assets could include the following elements:

- a colour (or colour combination)
- a logo or shape
- something with a face (a character or spokesperson)
- a sound (if audio media is part of the mix)
- a short phrase.

Set this palette as a long-term goal and start by building one or two first, and then add to them. Priorities should be assets that can be used on packaging and at the start of an advertisement, as these types of assets have additional benefits to the buyer and brand.

Conclusion

This chapter provided some simple steps to build a strong brand identity. Distilled from those steps are the following tactical dos and don'ts to help you build a strong brand identity.

- Do select a palette that taps in to different parts of the brain to give the brand identity neurological richness.
- Do measure the strength of the brand's distinctive assets—your judgement (and that of the marketing team) is likely to be overly optimistic.
- Do learn which distinctive assets help your brand to stand out in its shopping environment, and protect these with your life (or career)!
- Do think about all shopping environments when designing distinctive assets for packaging, including online, where packs are small and in two dimensions.
- Do make sure distinctive assets build consistency across all these areas:
    - executions in different media
    - campaigns over time
    - in-store and out-of-store activity
    - a parent brand and its variants.
  This ensures you always build rather than erode distinctive assets.
- Don't confuse distinctiveness with differentiation. These are separate; one is not a subset or replacement for the other.
- Don't choose a distinctive asset based on what it means to buyers; make the strongest meaning the brand name.
- Don't look to your (current) positioning for distinctive assets, as this is unlikely to be the best long-term decision for the brand's identity.
- Don't change your packaging unless you must, and realise that with this comes a need to re-educate category buyers.

- Don't assume you know how strong your distinctive assets are, as we all have a bias towards the brands we work with that blinds us. Robust, independent metrics help elevate the conversation from a clash of opinions to an evidence-based discussion of options.
- Don't stop using the strong assets—remember that non-use has a price, and that price is buyers' memory decay.

With a strategy in place to build a strong, neurologically diverse palette, distinctive assets can help accelerate a brand's mental and physical availability–building activities.

6

Achieving Reach

Jenni Romaniuk

Marketing activities need reach. Why? Because brand growth depends on the brand building its penetration (double jeopardy law), and recruiting a greater proportion of light category buyers (natural monopoly law). It's difficult to recruit category buyers you don't reach.

One aim of media strategy is to minimise the time gap between each purchase occasion and the last advertising exposure (for your brand). This means reaching all category buyers, and doing this as regularly as you can afford. Media fragmentation makes this an interesting challenge, as does the sheer complexity of media options. Add in the exploding world of mobile media and it is easy to get distracted from this goal of achieving reach by claims of exclusive audiences, engagement and proprietary metrics to assess effectiveness.

This chapter covers some broad fundamentals of media selection and scheduling in a fragmented environment. We present some simple knowledge that can make it easier to choose between the many different options available, even when the data on media usage is poor or lacks standardisation.

Welcome to the new media world

Marketing activities only build mental availability in the audience they reach. This makes planning for reach the foundation of any sound media strategy. The digital revolution ushers in more ways of reaching buyers, offering tantalising prospects of lower overall costs, better timing of exposure, even lower advertising avoidance. But achieving such outcomes is hardly straightforward. Every media opportunity seems to have some attractive features and some unattractive ones, with many options to choose from. Before we go into some guidelines for selecting media to achieve reach, let's first clarify what reach means (to us) and consider some of the persistent arguments against reach-based planning.

What does *reach* really mean?

The media planning industry has its own jargon, which surprisingly is seldom taught in marketing degrees. *Reach* refers to the size of the audience exposed to your marketing activity in a specific time period: for example, '40% 1+ reach' means that 40% of a particular population (say, 18–48-year-olds) in a specific time period in a particular geographic area receiving one or more (potential[1]) advertising exposures.

This is a simple metric but one unfortunately difficult to calculate across multiple media, as each tends to have its own measurement system. Most marketers live with knowing that, say, their television advertising achieved 65% reach while their newspaper advertising achieved 50% reach in the same period, with only a rough estimate of how much combined reach they achieved by advertising in both media.

---

1   With most media, it is never possible to guarantee that a person has really received an exposure, with advertising avoidance (for example, switching channels or using web ad-blockers) and lack of noticing of some exposures. Advertising 'exposures' are therefore often called 'opportunities to see' (OTS).

To reiterate, the importance of reach should be very obvious: a brand's marketing activity can only influence the category buyers[2] it reaches. Marketing activity that reaches a large proportion of category buyers *can* have a large sales impact, while an activity that reaches only a small group of people can, at best, only have a small sales impact.

Some basic maths reveals that if you lose (or plan for lower) reach, the extra response needed to achieve the same sales quickly becomes unachievable. For example, let's take the case of achieving 60% reach and having a 5% behavioural impact (this might be clicking or making an enquiry but, in this case, let's say it is placing an order). If the population is 1000 people, this combination will generate 30 sales (600 people × 0.05):

- if your reach is reduced to 40%, then you need 7.5% behavioural impact (that is, an extra 50% response) to achieve the same 30 sales (400 × 0.075)
- if your reach is halved, at 30%, then you need 10% behavioural impact (or 200% increase in response) to achieve the same 30 sales (300 × 0.1)
- if you focus on a low-reach activity, and only reach 10% of category buyers, then you need six times the baseline response (or a whopping 600% increase!) to achieve the same 30 sales (100 × 0.3).

Lower reach makes it harder to maintain the same sales level, let alone grow. While media plans can vary enormously in terms of the reach they generate—that is, you can buy more reach—rarely can they guarantee greater impact.

---

2   Sometimes word of mouth is put forward as a way to reach more people than planned for in the media schedule (this is discussed in Chapter 7).

But I can't plan for reach because ...

We still hear excuses to justify *not* having reach as the primary media objective. Here is the faulty logic of some of the most persistent reasons.

But the market is big and my budget is small

However large or small your budget, you want as much reach as your money will buy. Giving up on reach is one of the big reasons that brands don't grow.

Having a small budget means you can ill afford to waste it. Brands with (perceived) small budgets routinely do themselves harm by assuming that they cannot afford reach and therefore moving towards high cost per contact media: that is, trading reach for 'engagement'. This tendency (unnecessarily) gives bigger brands another advantage.

The real challenge for small brands is not that they can't afford reach; rather it's that their physical availability may be restricted. This means much of their advertising may reach buyers for whom the brand isn't easy to buy. Sometimes tinkering with the media or advertising is not the solution to getting more from advertising spend, but rather focusing instead on building physical availability.

But don't I need a frequency of at least three?

This is an old myth. Advertising isn't like a theoretical physics lecture; it doesn't need repeated viewings and much pondering before it finally sinks in. Good advertising works straight out of the gate and bad advertising[3] has little effect (no matter how many times it is seen).

Each and every exposure has an effect but additional nearby exposures don't have as much effect as the first one. This is intuitively obvious (once you know) and is supported by research on learning and a meta-analysis of laboratory experiments in cognitive psychology and marketing (Sawyer, Noel & Janiszewski, 2009). It also shows up in real-world single-source

---

3   Much bad advertising doesn't cause sales for a brand because it is working for other brands. Increasing the media weight is a dangerous way to attempt to fix this.

data: the first exposure within a time period has the greatest sales effect (Taylor, Kennedy & Sharp, 2009).

Not planning for reach and instead ending up with a small group of category buyers being hit by marketing activities two, three and more times is an inefficient use of the media budget.

Just because you can't reach all category buyers don't mean you shouldn't try. Studies into media consumption behaviour reveal why planning to reach as many category buyers as possible achieves better coverage (for example, see Sharp, Beal & Collins, 2009). Exposure patterns within and across media mean some people are simply easier to reach than others: they watch television more often, or are online more often and so wherever you schedule your marketing activity, they are easier to hit. If you don't plan to reach out to new buyers, excess frequency becomes the more likely natural outcome. This build-up of (less valuable) frequency reduces the return from your media budget as the second exposure costs the same as the first, but the return from two or more exposures is much lower.

My advertising message is sophisticated so people need to see it several times to get it

It is risky to draw on a multi-exposure advertising approach. For every lauded complex storyline campaign, there is a quickly buried raft of failures. Media fragmentation and consumption patterns make it difficult to schedule accurately for multiple, sequentially timed exposures to the same person.

But even if we could, why would we want to? Why take two or three exposures to achieve what could be achieved in one? This only makes sense if you are expecting at least two or three times the response level from those who do see it several times. Can your campaign guarantee this?

Successful advertising has a lingering effect on the category buyer brain, so any repeat-exposure within a short time frame is less efficient than reaching out to a new brain. The principle of one exposure media planning affects creativity as well—it means designing advertising that works first time, every time.

But surely I need to match my competitors' burst

Matching bad spending with similar bad spending is a recipe for both brands to be undercut by a smarter competitor. While bursts deliver reach in a short period of time, they also repeatedly hit heavier media consumers, which makes them a costly or inefficient way to reach light media consumers (Ceber, 2009). No brand can sustain a burst, and these bursts only affect people who are in the market at the time of or shortly after the burst. Unless you have a highly seasonal product (for example, 80% sold in a short period of time), even a successful burst will mean the brand lacks the on-air presence over the rest of the year when the majority of sales occur.

By planning for continuous reach, rather than mirroring competitors, you may lose slightly in a competitor's burst, but you will gain in the long term through greater impact when the competitor has to go off air.

No more excuses!

As you can see, there really is no excuse *not* to plan for reach if you want to use the media budget wisely. In all categories and markets, achieving reach is important. Even in emerging markets, with large populations, fragmented media systems and large influxes of new category buyers, reaching out to the wider category-buying population is of paramount importance if you want to have a chance at creating an economically sustainable brand.

Advertise where you sell

Plan for reach where you have, or want, physical availability. A key purpose of advertising is to build up mental availability, which nudges the buyer toward brand. Once this is achieved, physical availability then enables the buyer to easily act on that nudge. If physical availability is poor, then even excellent, wide-reaching advertising will not generate sales.

If you only distribute on the east coast of the USA or in Harbin in China, then advertising outside of these regions is of little value. In such cases, regional media might be a smart choice to avoid advertising in areas where people can't buy the brand—but only if the cost of regionalising your media strategy does not outweigh the benefits. If you want to sell to buyers to a new region in the near future, advertising builds everyone's mental availability for the brand, including retailers and distributors. This can help secure distribution.

(More) valuable audience: Light and non-brand buyers

In Chapter 2 we discussed how light and non-brand buyers matter most for brand growth. We therefore need to reach these buyers, mindful that they buy and notice the advertising of the other brands as well. Exposure to our advertising gives our brand a better chance of being salient in buying situations, through freshening memory and neutralising the effects of competitors' advertising exposures.

This makes media that reach lighter and non-brand buyers extremely valuable. Typically, this is media that reach most category buyers and, in doing so, also reach the ones whom you need for your brand to grow. But there are also three tactics that *reduce* the effectiveness of your media spend:

- *Making buyers work for exposure.* This tends to be low-reach or high-engagement media that make buyers engage in some way to qualify. It is only heavy brand buyers who are motivated to go this extra step. We see examples of this in Nelson-Field, Riebe and Sharp (2012) for Facebook fan pages, and Romaniuk, Beal and Uncles (2013) for a range of social media and events.
- *Make buyers work to identify your brand.* If the audience has to work hard to identify the brand, most won't; the few who do will be your past heavy brand buyers. You are left (only) preaching to the converted.
- *Unnecessary repetition.* A common mistake is to choose a large reach media vehicle, but then schedule spots to create extensive short-term duplication within that medium. For example, advertising in *NCIS* but buying multiple spots in the same show: this is only of value if you have a very different audience in each ad break—are you confident of that?

Avoid making category buyers work to achieve your advertising goals; light and non-buyers simply won't make that effort, and you therefore miss your most valuable audience for growth.

Don't neglect light and new category buyers

Strategies aimed predominantly at the brand's customer base—even when wide-reaching—can still miss an important group: light and new category buyers. When categories grow, any influx of new category buyers presents an opportunity for the brand. And even in mature categories, new category buyers enter as people go through life-stage changes.

New category buyers know very little about the category, and the brands within it. This means lower competition for mental availability, and brands that do make an impression at this nascent time have a 'blank-er' slate to can more easily establish a fresh brand in memory. Any media target should be broad enough to reach these buyers.

Choosing media platforms

Media scheduling should be buyer-centric, and this we know intuitively. The basic knowledge of *how many*, *how often*, *for how long* and *when* your category buyers consume different media is key to smart media planning. Unfortunately, we often lack robust buyer-centric media data to act on this intuition.

Luckily, media behaviour (across and within platforms) largely conforms to the law of double jeopardy. This means the *how often* and *for how long* directly correlate with *how many* (penetration) comprise the audience for the platform. Or put more simply, media that attract bigger audiences will be used more often and for longer by those audiences.

Figure 6.1 is from a sample of online users in Russia. We see the two most common media, going online with a personal computer and watching television, also have the most frequent users, with around 90% engaging in these activities on most days. In contrast, reading a magazine or going to the cinema have the double jeopardy double-whammy of the few people they do attract interacting less frequently.

Going online at an internet cafe is the obvious outlier in Figure 6.1; because it is something that only those without a computer do. A large proportion of the Russian internet-using population have computers, and so don't need to visit internet cafes. But those who do are active relatively frequently.

Figure 6.1: Media consumption habits of internet users in Russia 2014 (*n* = 800)

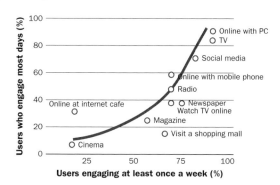

This application of law of double jeopardy means that, in the absence of other evidence, you can assume that high penetration media also attract their audience more often. But we do need to distinguish between a *medium* having large reach and a planner's ability to achieve extensive, unduplicated reach within that medium.

For example, in China in 2012, people reportedly spent more time on the internet than watching television (Meeker & Wu, 2013) but the internet is infinitely more fragmented than even television's 350-odd channels. While category buyers might spend more time online, fragmentation might make it difficult to schedule for cumulative reach.

The double jeopardy law also generally holds within a platform (that is, for different television channels, radio stations, similar genres of websites). Decades of evidence show this holding for television viewing patterns around the world (Sharp, Beal & Collins, 2009), and we have seen this extend to radio, online site visitation and so on. In Table 6.1 we show double jeopardy in social media site usage of online literate samples in China and the USA.

Table 6.1: Penetration and frequency of social media usage by internet users only—in China (2014) and the USA (2015)

Chinese sites	Users (%)	Highly active* users (%)	US sites	Users (%)	Highly active* users (%)
Wechat	96	88	Facebook	84	82
Qzone	93	75	Twitter	49	65
Youku	87	60	Google+	47	51
Sina Weibo	86	70	Instagram	41	64
Tencent Weibo	80	56	Pinterest	41	51
Renren	62	41	LinkedIn	38	34
Douban	59	39	Tumblr	25	50
PenYou	58	45	Vine	23	45
Kaixin 001	50	41	Flickr	18	39
51com	43	40	Ask.fm	17	47
Diandian	34	32	Tagged	15	56
Jiepang	32	30	Meetup	14	48
Average	**62**	**49**	**Average**	**34**	**53**

*Highly active = use most days

It is easy to check double jeopardy for the media platforms you are selecting between. Simply order the channels', sites', stations' or publications' penetration and frequency or volume figures by market share. A quick scatterplot visually shows the relationship.

Fragmentation, both within and across channels, makes the few properties able to attract large audiences particularly attractive. Once you have a large-reach property, adding a small-reach property in the same platform is rarely a good choice to build reach. Smaller media properties tend to attract heavy users of the medium, whom you have already reached with the other, larger reach, property. You achieve lots of duplication, and very little additional reach.

For example, let's look again at social media. The audience for smaller social media sites such as Pinterest comprises people who are active on more other social media sites, including the big ones such as Facebook and YouTube (see Table 6.2 for examples from Mexico and Nigeria). If you advertise or have a presence on a large social media site, advertising on a smaller social media sight is therefore of little value—spend your money elsewhere or at a different point in time.

Occasionally smaller media vehicles have higher than expected frequency or time spent viewing but, as they attract such a small audience, the overall eyeballs or ears contribution of that vehicle is typically small. These are often sold as attractive high-engagement media, but higher time spent or repeat exposures might not be good buys, as they generate excess frequency unless the repeat views are carefully spaced. Remember each exposure costs you the same, but close-together repeat exposures return less sales revenue.

Table 6.2: The repertoire size for social media and communications platforms by internet users in Mexico and Nigeria (2014)

Mexico	Penetration (%)	Number of other social media sites used by audience	Nigeria	Penetration (%)	Number of other social media sites used by audience
Facebook	91	2.1	Facebook	89	2.8
YouTube	84	2.3	WhatsApp	67	3.2
Twitter	45	3.2	YouTube	52	3.5
Instagram	21	4.2	Twitter	49	3.7
LinkedIn	14	4.3	LinkedIn	34	3.9
Badoo	10	5.1	Skype	22	4.1
Pinterest	8	5.6	Online Nigeria	20	3.8
Hi5	7	5.6	Instagram	15	4.8
Sonico	7	5.9	Pinterest	6	5.6
Metroflog	4	6.7	Tumblr	3	6.3
Average		**4.8**			**4.2**

The message is clear. First and foremost, choose media that attract a substantive audience. Then make sure you can cut through to reach category buyers in that medium.

Reach across touch-points in emerging markets

Media options now extend beyond the traditional television, print and radio to a wide range of digital, in-store and event properties. Even older media such as outdoor advertising are being invigorated with new technologies such as digital screens that change creative content or even speak to the passing audience.

Emerging markets demand an unprecedented level of flexibility in media planning that can extend from the most basic posters in local streets to sophisticated mobile platforms. With such a diverse tool kit, understanding how these touch-points might interact to help or hinder achieving reach in a cross-platform media plan is important.

As an illustrative example, we examined the reach of touch-points across six emerging markets (China, Turkey, Thailand, Vietnam, Taiwan and Malaysia) from a series of surveys for a personal-care category in 2012. In each country, category buyers were asked if they had seen or heard key brands across 17 touch-points ranging from traditional media such as television and radio, to in-store and online activities such as the brand's website or social media.

We summed the reach across brands for each touch-point, and ranked these touch-points from highest to lowest. The results (Table 6.3) show remarkable similarity in the top five touch-points across countries: product or pack on shelf; television advertising; supermarket flyers or coupons; price promotions or bonus packs; and free gift with purchase. This list highlights that, while new media is exciting, the basics of traditional media and in-store activities are also vital to achieve reach in the fragmented media environment that characterises emerging markets.

Exceptions for specific countries or touch-points may be leveraged, provided the main strategy was on track. These are some examples of differences we found in this personal-care category:

- social media was higher ranked in China
- supermarket flyers or coupons were lower ranked in Malaysia
- peer/in-store promoter recommendation ranked higher in Taiwan
- print advertising (newspapers and magazines) ranked higher for Thailand and Taiwan.

Table 6.3: Touch-points in a personal-care category ranked by reach achieved across key brands in five emerging markets (2012)

Ranked by average across countries	China	Taiwan	Thailand	Turkey	Vietnam
Product or pack on shelf	1st	2nd	1st	1st	1st
Television advertising	2nd	1st	2nd	4th	2nd
Supermarket flyers or catalogues	4th	4th	3rd	2nd	3rd
Price promo or bonus packs	3rd	9th	4th	3rd	4th
Free gift with purchase	6th	6th	6th	5th	5th
Peer recommendation	10th	3rd	10th	6th	6th
In-store promoter advice	8th	10th	7th	7th	7th
Print advertising	13th	5th	5th	13th	9th
In-store demos	11th	7th	11th	8th	8th
Outdoor advertising	14th	8th	9th	15th	10
Expert recommendation	15th	11th	8th	10th	11th
Radio advertising	12th	14th	12th	14th	12th
Free samples	17th	12th	13th	9th	14th
PR events	9th	13th	14th	17th	13th
Social media	5th	17th	16th	12th	16th
Mobile (SMS/MMM/App)	7th	15th	17th	16th	17th
Internet advertising	16th	16th	15th	11th	15th

Mixing a media cocktail

Sometimes you saturate a media channel, and achieving additional short-term reach means paying for considerable additional frequency. Then you have two options: save the money for the next time period or add another medium to the mix. Similar to adding spots, when adding media platforms, achieving unduplicated reach is the priority.

People consume multiple, different media. Given the paucity of buyer-centric data, how do we plan for unduplicated reach when incorporating multiple platforms?

We can draw on the duplication of purchase law from Chapter 3, which was actually first discovered in television viewing behaviour (Goodhardt & Ehrenberg, 1969). Applying this analysis across media or within media or both can help direct media choices (Redford, 2005). There are two points of particular of interest:

- excess audience sharing—which highlights media pairs to avoid, due to higher than expected duplication if both media options are chosen
- deficits in sharing—which will highlight media pairs that together might help achieve more unduplicated reach.

Table 6.4 shows media audience sharing from China. It shows every other media channel shares around 80% of its audience with television, the biggest channel. But the other options presented have different sharing levels for different media. We now highlight a couple of these findings and how they can help inform media planning.

Table 6.4 shows that, in China, video ads via social media share more audience members with supermarket flyers/coupons, outdoor events, mobile and SMS advertising, and radio. These combinations are likely to lead to higher audience duplication in a multi-platform campaign. In contrast, the overlap in audiences was substantively lower for free giveaways, in-store promoter advice, peer word of mouth and in-store advertising. These multi-platform combinations are therefore less likely to lead to audience duplication. While the result of this type of analysis is only one input when designing a multi-platform campaign, as timing and costs also need to be factored in, however this can highlight more fruitful combinations, worth exploring further.

Table 6.4: Sharing audiences across media in China (2012) (selected results)

Of those who were reached in the following media	Total reached (%)	Were also reached by (%)			
		Television ads	Social media video ads	Instore promoter advice	Peer word of mouth
Television ads	62	—	40	20	17
Social media video ads	31	80	—	7	5
Supermarket flyers/coupons	27	77	63	22	17
Free gifts/giveaways	22	83	18	44	36
Outdoor booths/events	17	84	81	16	12
In-store promoter advice	16	77	13	—	46
Ads via SMS or mobile	16	90	82	13	9
Ads for brands in-store	15	78	9	58	46
Peer word of mouth	13	85	12	58	—
Radio	10	89	84	15	9
Average	16	83	40	20	17

Figures in **bold** show excess sharing. Shaded figures show deficits in sharing.

The tactical routes to achieve maximum unduplicated reach are always going to vary. It's like making a good stir-fry: if you have the sound basic principles of a hot wok and oil with a high smoking point, you can mix any number of meat, vegetable and sauce combinations to get a great dish. These are some basic principles to remember for a good media mix:

- television is an invaluable part of any media mix, as many examples show (Binet & Field, 2009; Rubinson, 2009). So don't abandon or avoid it lightly.
- aim for the biggest reach medium first, and then only add to this if you achieve more unduplicated reach than duplicated reach in that week (Sharp et al., 2014)

- look at media in different families, as this is more likely to lead to higher unduplicated reach (Romaniuk, Beal & Uncles, 2013). For example, mix television with digital and in-store, rather than two digital or in-store properties.

Conclusion

Building mental availability is underpinned by a sound media strategy, the foundation of which is reach. While today's fragmented media world and the complexity of today's global markets can make achieving reach seem daunting, we provide some rules to simplify media choices.

- *First*: prioritise the audience for brand growth, which is light and non-brand buyers. These category buyers will largely be found in big-reach media. If in a growing category, look to reach light *category* buyers.
- *Second*: draw upon the law of double jeopardy to understand that small media properties tend to attract heavy media users, who are also found viewing larger media properties. Unless you can be assured of unduplicated reach, assume any investment in small media properties is likely to produce more frequency than reach.
- *Third*: when looking to engage in a multi-platform campaign, examine audience sharing across media options via duplication analysis to uncover more fruitful cross-platform avenues to explore.

7

Word-of-Mouth Facts Worth Talking About

Jenni Romaniuk and Robert East

W ord of mouth (WOM) is treated as the superman of media—
it's free, powerful and gives any brand the ability to leap bigger
brands in a single campaign. Initially popular in the 1960s, WOM lost
favour to other forms of influence, until last decade's surge in social media
prompted a renaissance. More people with more opportunities to share
about brands—now that's something to talk about! Ask people, and they
will tell you that WOM is important to them but does being (perceived
as) important to buyers make it equally important to marketers?

WOM has particular resonance in emerging markets, because it seems
like a cure-all to two issues that plague marketers in these countries. First,
many emerging markets score highly as collectivist cultures, where people
express a greater desire to fit in with family and friends, leading to claims
that WOM is more influential than in other countries. The second issue
is the challenge of media fragmentation, combined with social media,
creating more opportunities for category buyers to access and share ideas
with peers.

WOM's kryptonite is the lack of control marketers have, which makes harnessing its power difficult. In this chapter we cover knowledge to help you to assess, focus and manage WOM activities sensibly as part of the larger media mix. We point out the strengths and limitations of WOM, and provide the knowledge to give all-important context to WOM metrics.

The lure of word of mouth

Once upon a time a brand became very big, purely through the power of word of mouth. Its buyers loved it so much they talked of it non-stop to their family, friends and anyone they happened to meet. As the word spread, more people bought the brand and they too told their family, friends, work colleagues and schoolmates, until gradually the brand was the number one in its category all over the country. The brand's manager got promoted and everyone lived happily ever after …

Sounds like a fairy tale? Well, that is because it largely is. WOM can be a useful addition to the marketing and media mix, when harnessed correctly—but it is not the saviour that its (many) evangelists suggest. It's a small part of a big-picture brand-growth strategy. Myths about WOM's power often blind marketers to smart implementation and lead to inefficient allocation of resources through paying too much attention to trivialities.

It is easy to see the attraction of WOM as a panacea to having small budgets in large, populous countries. For emerging markets, some commentators even go further to claim that WOM is even more powerful than in the developed world, as the reported collectivist nature of many emerging markets means buyers place more value on the advice of family, friends and colleagues.

Vague statistics are often used to support this claim, so look a bit more closely before trusting any findings. For example, McKinsey consultants claim that more people in emerging markets received recommendations about food and beverage categories before making purchases; and more Chinese consumers said they would consider recommendations from family and friends about moisturiser compared to US consumers (Atsmon & Magni, 2012). While these types of statements are easy to accept, as they support the prevailing view, this is hardly strong evidence. Receiving or considering WOM is not the same as acting upon the advice[1]!

WOM routinely heads the list of sources that buyers self-report as important, and often-quoted statistics talk about the large volume of conversations that are about brands on a daily basis. But these statistics give a misleading picture of importance. First, we have a self-selection bias; we like to think we aren't fools swayed by advertising, and saying our purchase was based on advice from someone else is a more comfortable explanation. Second, while there are many conversations about brands, there are many more people and many more brands than conversations. We will show how many of these conversations don't reach the necessary people to influence brand purchases.

That is not to say WOM is inconsequential. A large number of inexperienced buyers or buyers faced with major decisions might turn to WOM for guidance on choices. Indeed WOM has a long history as influential in new product adoption, particularly for disruptive innovations where more buyers need to directly hear about or see the product in action before buying[2]. But again, this is different from the effect of WOM on routine purchases or for existing products and categories.

---

1   The lack of strong evidence is probably why the collectivist stereotype is not universally accepted, with some arguing that the need for fitting in and approval from close family and friends is a personal, rather than country, characteristic.

2   For more background, see Bass and King (1968).

To use WOM effectively, you need to vaccinate yourself against myths. Currently many actions about WOM are built on the shaky foundations of many unsupported beliefs. In this chapter we dispel myths and provide evidence across a range of areas fundamental to good WOM practice, such as incidence, the impact of WOM and the interpretation of WOM metrics.

One characteristic of WOM is that it often has a valence, or direction, in that it is positive or negative for the brand. This leads to our first question: which is more important, positive or negative WOM?

Should I focus on positive or negative WOM?

Allocating resources (attention, staff, money) on the most important areas is the first step to designing a smart strategy. WOM is often characterised in terms of valence: the positive, which is when someone says something good about the brand; and the negative, which is when someone says something damaging about the brand. Some WOM is a neutral statement of fact (such as the store is open until 8 p.m.) without a particular valence, but let's put that aside for now.

For the most part, positive WOM is good for the brand and negative WOM is bad for the brand[3], so how much time or resources should you spend building up or encouraging positive WOM versus stopping or dealing with the fall out from negative WOM?

To answer this question, let's first dispel a common myth that negative WOM is more common than positive WOM: the evidence tells us otherwise. Positive WOM is much more common than negative WOM (East, Hammond & Wright, 2007). Figure 7.1 shows this for mobile phone handsets across ten countries, where positive WOM is two to five times more common than negative WOM.

---

3 A small amount of WOM has cross-effects—whereby positive WOM from someone from whom you have differing tastes could lead you to be less likely to buy the recommended or whose negative WOM could pique curiosity and lead to a higher probability of brand purchase—but this is usually confined to a small amount (around 3%) and to a few specific categories such as television programs, movies or fashion items.

Figure 7.1: Relative levels of positive to negative WOM for mobile phone handsets (2014)

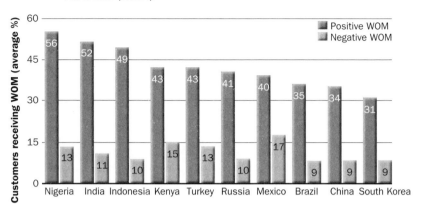

Even commonly talked about categories such as restaurants and movies, or high-priced categories such as cars follow this pattern (see Figure 7.2). The volume of positive WOM is around three times higher than negative WOM, similar to the averages reported in East, Hammond and Wright (2007).

Figure 7.2: Comparison of volumes of positive and negative WOM across three categories in USA and China

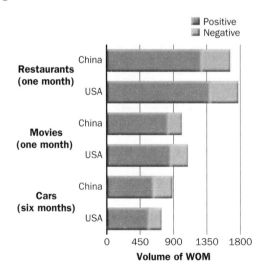

The greater volume for positive WOM is simply because more people give or receive positive WOM, at a slightly higher rate, than they do for negative WOM (see Table 7.1 for three categories in the USA and China). Negative WOM spreads at much the same rate or a slightly lower one than positive WOM.

Table 7.1: Positive and negative WOM for three categories in China and the USA (2014)

Category and country	Respondents receiving at least one WOM incident (%)*		Frequency* (base = those giving WOM)	
	Positive WOM	Negative WOM	Positive WOM	Negative WOM
Restaurants—China	62	28	3.5	2.2
Restaurants—USA	76	31	3.1	1.9
Movies—China	55	16	2.5	1.8
Movies—USA	57	18	2.6	2.0
Cars—China	47	21	2.2	2.0
Cars—USA	42	15	2.1	1.8
Average	57	22	2.7	1.7

*Time frame = one month for restaurants and movies, six months for cars

Why is positive WOM more common? Well, to give negative WOM, you need a story. Most brands work as they should, so they don't provide anything worthy of (negative) conversation. This reduces the pool of people available to produce negative WOM. Many more people are in the market to give positive WOM. And positive WOM is more useful, as people typically gain more value from advice on what to select rather than what to avoid.

Another fear is that negative WOM is inherently more powerful than positive WOM—it has more influence on recipients. This is also a myth. East and Hammond (2006) provide comprehensive, multi-category evidence that positive and negative WOM have largely the same effect.

Positive WOM is more influential on the brand's sales—reaching many more people with largely the same effect as negative WOM. Unless your brand is performing poorly (and in which case, fix the brand first!), don't dwell too much on negative WOM.

WOM equals conversation (about brands)

We call it *word of mouth*, which makes it easy to lose sight of the fact that for normal people, this is called *conversation*. Remember: most WOM is shared between people who have a personal relationship. The idea that everyone is seeking the advice of strangers is largely a myth. For example, in a 2014 survey we conducted in China, across three categories we found that 85% of WOM was from work colleagues, family members and friends. Only 15% of WOM was from people not very well known to the recipient.

For someone to receive WOM, someone else has to give it. That WOM occurs largely between people who are well known to each other means that the giver knows something of the interests and tastes of the people to whom they are talking, which shapes the direction of any conversation, including that about brands. When we converse with strangers, we test topics to discover mutual interests but with family and friends we are pre-informed and so we know what to talk about (and what not to).

Why do people talk about brands?

Jenni would like to share a story. The last time she was in Shanghai, she went to this great restaurant—Lost Heaven … now from here, there are two ways to go.

- Jenni can tell you how great the food was, and how it was great value for money—now some of you have drifted off and stopped paying attention (please come back!), because you are not in Shanghai, have never been and have no plans to go. With this direction, her only interested audience are those currently in Shanghai, those who have been or those who are going in the near future.

- Jenni can tell you how it was fascinating to see the Burmese influence in the food because of how close Burma is to China, and talk about the recent political shifts in Burma, and China's influence in the region. Oh, and she might slip in the food was delicious and great value too. In which case she has kept the Shanghainese, and the past and future visitors interested, but also those interested in the region generally, political history and a wide range of interests. The reason is that the brand is part of the story, not the whole story. Indeed some of those people interested in the region might end up in Shanghai, and now they have a restaurant recommendation for when they visit.

We often assume that a brand's actions are the primary triggers for WOM but this is only part of the explanation. People also give WOM because they perceive it to be helpful to the recipient, or it just came up in conversation (East et al., 2015; Mangold, Miller & Brockway, 1999). The brand can place itself in line for WOM by its actions but it is the situation of the giver that influences the actual delivery.

Understanding the full range of motives for giving WOM tells us the giver acts as a gatekeeper, picking the people to share any specific piece of information. This constrains the reach of WOM as givers only give if *they perceive* the WOM will be of value to the recipient—either because they know that person is in the market to buy, or because the story is interesting or enjoyable (and so improves the conversation). Why give WOM if it doesn't have currency in the conversation?

This means conversation-worthy stories about the brand are particularly valuable, as they can be shared without an explicit need to know someone is in the market for a category or brand. Without a story to share, the giver is likely wait for an external motivation to stimulate the WOM, such as someone indicating through their conversation they are in the market or a direct request for advice. Interesting stories allow the brand's WOM to circumvent those conversational conventions.

Marketers need to think about what brand stories are sufficiently compelling to be sharable in a conversation. It also means to consistently generate WOM, you need to provide fresh stories to pass on as people are unlikely to (deliberately) repeat the same story to the same people.

If your marketing plan is relying on WOM to drive purchase, consider how you can deal with these issues, and the next point which is that people usually give WOM about brands they have experienced.

Experience with the brand matters

Experience gives us the stories to tell. People usually give WOM about brands when they have firsthand experience. Figure 7.3 shows examples, taken from East, Romaniuk and Lomax (2011), of givers of WOM from South Korea and Lebanon, as well as averages across fifteen categories in a range of developed and emerging markets. Positive WOM tends to be given by current users of the brand (East, Romaniuk & Lomax, 2011), as these buyers are more likely to meet these conditions:

- have formed a (confident) opinion about a brand;
- have seen the brand's advertising (Romaniuk & Wight, 2009); and
- have had an unusual brand experience/story to share.

Figure 7.3: (a) Positive and (b) negative WOM examples

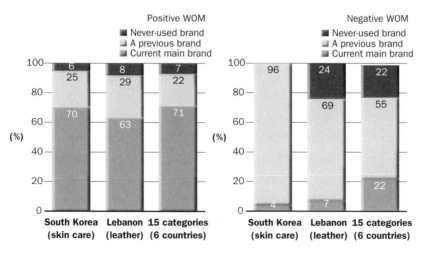

Source: East, Romaniuk & Lomax, 2011

In contrast, the brand's lapsed users or defectors give more negative WOM, as they:

- are most likely to have a negative experience to share; or
- generate negative feelings to rationalise their defection from the brand (Winchester, Romaniuk & Bogomolova, 2008).

Current brand users thus dominate positive WOM, while lapsed users and defectors dominate negative WOM. Very little WOM is generated from those who lack experience with the brand. This makes over-reliance on WOM a risky option for new brands, without many experienced customers, to rely on.

This correlation between defection and the giving of negative WOM highlights a key limitation of the *net promoter score* (Reichheld, 2003), which only captures willingness to give WOM from the brand's current customers. This can't capture negative WOM generated by brand defectors and so under-represents negative WOM (East, Romaniuk & Lomax, 2011).

Relax—your WOM is probably normal

Like most brand-level metrics, WOM levels are highly correlated with market share (Uncles, East & Lomax, 2010). Brands with a larger share receive more positive WOM than smaller brands. Figure 7.4 illustrates this for major banks in Indonesia and Russia, where larger banks, such as Sberbank in Russia and Central Asia Bank in Indonesia, have more people receiving positive WOM than their smaller counterparts. Therefore a small brand will typically have less WOM than a big brand, just simply because it has fewer people with sufficient experience to express an opinion.

Figure 7.4: Brands receiving positive WOM for banks in (a) Indonesia and (b) Russia (2014)

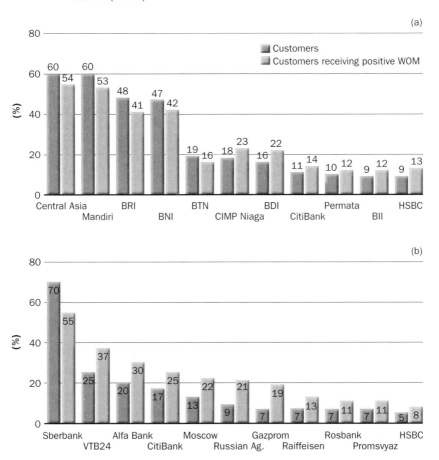

We see this relationship for the same brand across multiple countries, as illustrated with HSBC in Figure 7.5. In Brazil and China, where HSBC has more personal banking customers, positive WOM is higher than in Russia where the brand has fewer customers.

A brand's share or usage level should set your expectations about WOM levels relative to other brands in the category. It is therefore possible to determine if the brand's levels of WOM are higher, lower or as expected for its size, rather than naively relying on the raw percentages. This is particularly useful for managers of global brands, when comparing across countries where the brand differs in share.

Figure 7.5: Relationship between number of customers and incidence of positive WOM for HSBC across six countries (2014)

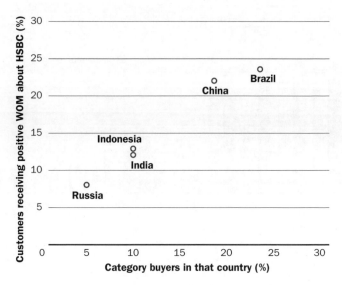

Positive WOM has the most influence when ...

The effect of a particular piece of advice depends on how likely the recipient was to buy the brand *prior to receiving the advice* (East, Hammond & Lomax, 2008). Without understanding the recipients' baseline probability of buying, it is easy to overestimate the effect of WOM on sales.

As Chapter 1 showed, the normal distribution of a brand's buying propensity looks like the reverse J in Figure 7.6, with lots of people with little or no propensity to buy the brand in the future.

What about those receiving WOM—how likely are they to buy the brand before hearing the WOM? Let's take positive WOM for cars in the USA as an example. Those who had received recent positive WOM about a car brand in the last six months were asked about their probability of buying that brand before and after receipt[4]. The difference between the two is the impact, and in this case we see that positive WOM lifts the

---

4   Survey was conducted in November 2014 amongst 600 respondents in China; this
     approach is the same as used in East, Hammond and Lomax (2008).

Figure 7.6: Probability of considering Citibank for next banking product across India, China and Brazil 2014

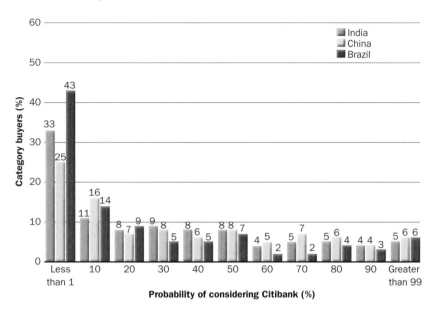

probability of buying a car brand by an average of +0.9 percentage points (no surprise here, but reassuring!).

But is it the same lift across everyone? To test this, we plotted the impact for each probability of buying the car brand before receiving the WOM to see if it varied (see Figure 7.7). We also include the percentage of people at each probability level (from zero to 100), as this is crucial to contexualise the impact figures, as high impact on few people will still have only small overall return for the brand.

From Figure 7.7, several key findings become apparent:

- positive WOM has its greatest impact when it reaches those with a lower propensity (one or two chances out of ten) to buy the brand—this is more than double the average effect size.
- a mismatch exists between where the people are, and where impact peaks: 63% of people reached by positive WOM already had a 70% or more probability of buying the brand. At a probability of 70 or 80%, the impact halves to around 0.4.

Figure 7.7: Incidence and impact[5] of positive WOM for cars in the USA (2015)

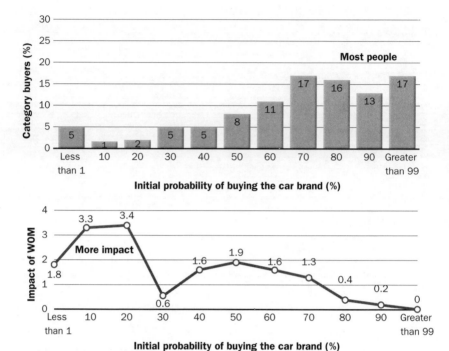

- the very low probability group (close to zero or one) contains a few genuine brand rejectors who resist positive WOM.
- the audience for positive WOM skews to those with a high propensity to buy the brand, which needs to be taken into account when quantifying the effect of WOM.

This is not to dismiss the value of positive WOM reaching people with a higher prior probability of purchase, but rather to highlight that the return on investment (ROI) of WOM from these people is lower than it could be if the WOM reached people with a lower propensity.

WOM for cars in China follows similar patterns (Figure 7.8). Impact is highest amongst low, but not zero probability buyers of the brand; most recipients have a higher probability of buying, but WOM has more impact

---

5   Calculated as the difference between probabilities of purchasing a brand before and after receipt of WOM

amongst low-propensity buyers. Cars are still quite a new category for many buyers in China, which is why the distribution is not as skewed to high propensity as it is in the USA.

Figure 7.8: Incidence and impact of positive WOM for cars in China (2014)

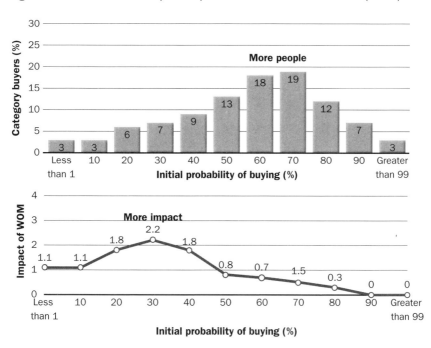

WOM's distribution is in the hands (mouths) of the givers, who look to talk to people whom they perceive have an interest in the category or brand. This skews the audience for WOM to those with an established interest. Calculations of the effect of WOM on sales need to account for this higher baseline, as does ROI modelling that compares WOM with other media without a skewed audience, such as television advertising.

What about the impact of negative WOM?

For negative WOM, the pattern reverses, with the biggest influence on those who have a high propensity to buy the brand (see Figure 7.9 for an example from restaurants in China where the average effect of negative WOM is a drop of 1.3 scale points). The effect is virtually zero for those who have low propensity to buy the brand, and is greatest amongst those with a propensity of nine out of ten or more (90% or greater).

Figure 7.9: Incidence and impact[6] of negative WOM for restaurants in China 2014

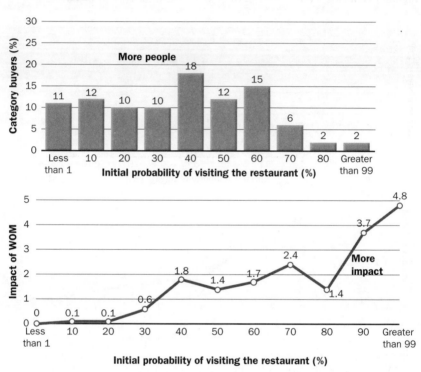

When negative WOM reaches someone with a high propensity to buy the brand, it can have a large effect: it just rarely reaches these people. This stifles the overall effect of negative WOM. We thus see a mismatch in audience and impact, which curtails the possible impact of WOM. Both positive and negative WOM *can* have a big impact, but both tend to *fail to reach the right people* to do this. This highlights an issue with many market mix or ROI models that don't factor in the prior propensity of

---

6   Sign of impact is positive for convenience for the charts, but negative WOM stimulated a drop in propensity to buy the brand.

the audience reached, and that it might be positively skewed to heavy brand buyers. If this is not taken into account, it is easy to overstate the importance of small reach media with a skew to existing heavy brand buyers.

And the idea that WOM might have more influence in emerging markets than in the developed world? To test this we did an 'apples with apples' comparison between the USA and China, with similarly sourced internet panel samples across three categories, quantifying the effect of positive and negative WOM.

We compared the overall impact (see Figure 7.10), as well as the impact on only those who reported an initial probability of five out of ten (50%), to compare those who can equally move higher or lower in response to WOM (Figure 7.11).

The results show no evidence that WOM has more impact in China. We also don't see any evidence that negative WOM has more impact than positive WOM (consistent with East & Hammond, 2006). For people with equal room to move, the impact of advice (positive or negative) is very similar: in the USA, average positive WOM impact = +2.3 and negative WOM impact = –2.1; in China, positive WOM impact = +1.2; negative WOM impact = –1.3.

Figure 7.10: Comparison of overall impact of WOM: China versus the USA (2014–15)

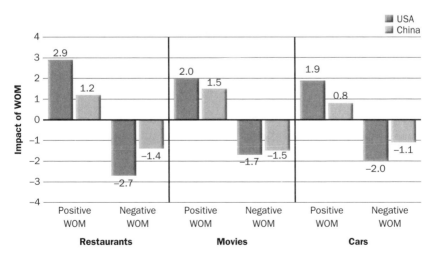

Figure 7.11: Comparison of impact of WOM: China versus the USA—only those with a prior purchasing probability of five out of ten (50%) (2014–15)

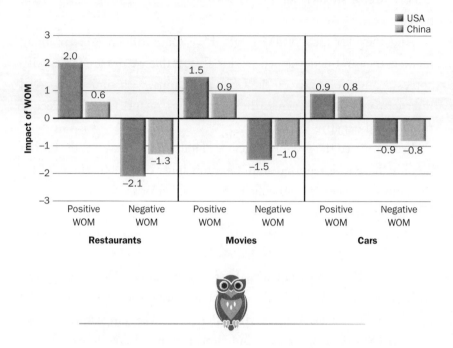

WOM as a reinforcer

While the skewed audience for positive WOM limits its influence as an acquisition force, WOM does the helpful job of reminding the giver of brands previously bought. While the receiver of a tweet might pay it scant attention, the composer of the tweet spent effort creating that message; while the receiver of advice about a car might be daydreaming while the giver was talking, the giver was dredging their long-term memory and remembering past experiences to provide their advice. We should not neglect the power of WOM to remind the giver of how they feel about the brand. If this WOM is positive (which it largely will be), it can help the brand secure future sales from existing customers.

In repertoire categories, when advertising activity is low or when the brand is not obviously present in the environment, it is easy for the buyer to forget previously bought brands. The act of expressing WOM to others is an internal reminder, in effect acting as a self-generated 'advertising-like' exposure. For high involvement or visible purchases, giving positive WOM can help reassure the buyer of a decision made.

Don't neglect this impact of WOM; it's hard to measure but is useful to include in any reach calculations that, in giving WOM, the giver is also 'reached' by that same WOM.

Conclusion

WOM is an attractive source of promotion for brands, and our results show how to sensibly take advantage of the opportunities that WOM presents, without over-investing.

The strong correlations with market share give marketers a context for interpreting a brand's WOM levels: there's no need to panic if you have a small brand and low levels of WOM; and don't get excited if you are a large brand with higher positive WOM levels—these results are normal.

Negative WOM is rarely worthy of attention. It is uncommon and lacks influence. Don't be distracted by it unless something is new or the brand undergoes a major change, such as a product reformulation.

Positive WOM has the most effect when it reaches those with a low or medium propensity to buy the brand. Stories or talking points that have a broad conversation value will help givers spread the word to a wider audience. Taking into account the propensity to buy the brand prior to receiving the WOM is crucial to avoid overestimating the sales effects of WOM. But don't also neglect the value of WOM as a reinforcing form of self-generated advertising that reminds givers of their positive brand experiences.

Surprisingly, given the rhetoric on the power of WOM emerging markets, our results for WOM in emerging markets mirror findings for the developed world, so we see no reason to change WOM strategy in these countries.

Finally, a reality check: advertising is often considered WOM's less attractive sibling—less memorable, less effective. But WOM has the same cut-through issues as advertising. Even WOM via social media suffers from this—just try it sometime: post something about a brand on whatever social network you use, and then find out how many people in your network actually saw it.

Peer-to-peer WOM is a capricious element to harness, and investing substantially in this at the expense of media where you can control content and distribution is a big risk.

8

Building Physical Availability

Magda Nenycz-Thiel, Jenni Romaniuk and Byron Sharp

This chapter is the first of two that cover the vitally important area of physical availability. The core of physical availability is about making the brand *easy to find and buy*. It's about identifying and removing the speed bumps, no matter how small, between having the brand mentally available and actual purchase. Without physical availability, investments in building mental availability will be largely wasted.

We have split physical availability into three dimensions: *presence*, which covers decisions on where to place the brand, such as channel and retailer choice; *relevance*, which covers decisions about the portfolio options; and *prominence*, which is about making the brand easily found in its shopping environments.

In the next chapter, Chapter 9, we focus on e-commerce.

What makes something 'easy to buy'?

Regardless of whether the market is developed, emerging or somewhere in between, it is an obvious, but often neglected fact, that if a brand is not available, it can't be bought. The positive relationship between brand distribution and market share shows smaller share brands have lower distribution and sell less per point of retail distribution than larger share brands (Wilbur & Farris, 2013).

Channels are proliferating. This is particularly evident in emerging markets, which often retain a strong traditional trade and have a growing modern (supermarket-style) trade, while leapfrogging into the internet and mobile e-commerce age with sites such as taobao.com offering everything from high-end luxury goods to everyday household food products. But even in the developed world, e-commerce and m-commerce (mobile commerce) expand ways to make any product or service physically available.

More options are a double-edged sword, as with each choice that expands physical availability comes (quickly expanding) channel costs. Given that popular outlets will contain many competitive offerings, getting presence is only half the battle. Further effort is needed to maximise the value from the presence within each location, otherwise mental availability–building efforts are wasted as the category buyer selects a competitor instead. These challenges mean physical availability is often under-leveraged. This is an opportunity for marketers who get serious about this as a core part of brand strategy.

This chapter lays the foundations for creating an easy-to-buy brand. We draw on a framework of three components—presence, relevance and prominence (Figure 8.1)—to encourage you to think holistically about building physical availability.

Figure 8.1: Three components of physical availability

Presence: Is your brand where it needs to be?

Presence is the backbone of physical availability as it holds everything else in place. In today's fragmented, multi-channel environment, it is usually impossible to cover all possible buying locations. Poor decisions can lead to missed opportunities or quickly ramp up costs—so how do you decide on the best option(s)?

A thorough understanding of shopping behaviour is first step. Know where and when category buyers shop, and how and when these outlets compete with each other. Aim to place your brand in channels and outlets to cover as many different buying occasions as possible. Put simply, you want to minimise the odds that someone buying the category can't find your brand. Remember, buyers typically have repertoires of brands, even in traditionally solely loyal markets such as financial services, insurance and telecommunications. If your brand is mentally available but not physically available, another brand is easily substituted.

It's important that a brand's physical availability overlaps with its mental availability. If a brand is well known in the North but only well distributed in the South, the negative sales consequences of this mismatch are obvious, these two market-based assets aren't working together. While this sounds obvious the degree of overlap is seldom measured and therefore seldom managed by companies.

Managing this overlap is particularly important when launching a new brand, or entering a market. Ideally a brand needs to grow mental and physical availability in perfect synchronisation, which is to say amongst the same buyers. Mismatches are common early on in a brand's life and they reduce the effectiveness of the marketing spend enormously. This consideration may mean there is benefit in launching first in a defined geographic area if it is also possible to buy media that is restricted to that area. This makes it easier to manage the mental and physical availability overlap, it also may reduce the cost and risk of a launch.

Another tactic is to start broad reach advertising a little before rolling out physical availability. Obviously this comes at some cost (expenditure when no sales revenue is coming in) but it helps ensure that product does not sit on shelves, and therefore risk delisting, in the early stages of launch.

Expanding logistics when you have a physical product can be expensive but not being where the customer is buying means lost sales. Adding channels and retailers increases the coverage of category-buying occasions, but each addition needs to be weighed against the cost of establishing and managing a brand's presence in that new channel or retailer. With services it is a little easier, but there are still additional costs and challenges in managing multiple channels, particularly if brokers or technology interfaces are involved. We also need to distinguish between sales channels and servicing channels.

Grocery: Channelling choice

If we understand how people shop across outlets, we can better prioritise outlets for the brand. In the developed world, developed systems mean a well-trodden path with established supermarket retailers. While not immune to change, with the growth of online and mobile commerce providing opportunities to bypass supermarkets and sell directly to customers (discussed in more detail in Chapter 9), the vast majority of grocery shopping is conducted in conventional supermarkets.

Emerging markets present a particular challenge for channel management for several reasons:

- the sheer size of the markets (both in population and geography) makes central distribution locations inefficient, while multiple distribution locations add to costs and complexity
- the rapidly increasing presence of supermarkets and hypermarkets require training of both shoppers and distributors
- the residual strong traditional trade presence, particularly in rural areas
- the emergence of online shopping to further fragment channel options
- the reliance on many small local stores (often referred to as extended pantries) to provide a source of spur-of-the-moment replacement purchases, as most homes have minimal storage.

This all adds up to a diverse and complex system of potential physical availability paths.

At what point is the additional distribution adding costs but not any major value? Knowing where to be, to reach potential buying occasions, is crucial for both smart investment and growth.

Achieving market coverage

In Chapter 3 we discussed how, within a category, brands sell to very similar types of buyers. Spending time and effort to identify and target a special sort of customer for your brand is therefore of little value—you should target all category buyers instead. Here we consider a similar question for physical availability: do different channels or retailers sell to different types of shoppers?

Previous research in the UK has found grocers, music outlets and high street shops all sell to similar profiles of shoppers (Kennedy & Ehrenberg, 2001). Given today's expanding retail options—the increasing role of online and mobile, and the complicated channel structures of today's emerging markets—are some channels overweighted to a particular, important demographic you can't reach elsewhere?

The answer to this question is yes, sometimes, because the retailing environment largely dictates how people shop. Convenience matters: people generally shop in ways that are *easy to access*, just they buy brands that are easy to find. When a channel is difficult to get to, people don't use it but this shopping behaviour can easily change when the retail landscape changes.

For example, in South Africa, Spaza and Township stores are located in areas populated by people with lower income and education levels. These catchment qualities are then reflected in Spaza and Township store customer bases, with few of these lower income shoppers visiting supermarkets.

What would happen if a supermarket opened in that same location?

Well this actually happened in Soweto, a lower income community in Johannesburg. Before 2010, Spaza and Township stores were the only place to buy groceries. The closest mall with supermarkets was an hour's drive away, which meant that the majority of shopper needs were satisfied by local options. Then the Maponya Mall opened in 2010, and it offered Pick 'n' Pay and other supermarkets to grocery shoppers in this location. How did shopping behaviour change?

Soweto shoppers did not replace Spaza outlets with Pick 'n' Pay—these shoppers are still highly likely to shop at Spaza outlets (60%). But two years on, Pick 'n' Pay's penetration in Soweto is comparable to the much wealthier suburb Johannesburg South (Soweto: 69%; Johannesburg South: 70%; 2012 figures from National Advertising Bureau Roots survey). Soweto shoppers added the new options to their channel repertoires and now shop at more channels. Pick 'n' Pay, now *accessible*, is one of those channels.

The accessibility of an outlet plays a more important role than its type. Coverage means reaching people in different locations, so it is useful to know what type of people live in a particular area, rather than be too concerned about which type of people currently shop at a supermarkets or other channels. Anyone will shop at a channel or retailer (sometimes), but only if they have access to them!

This makes internet access important when trying to define the e-commerce customer, particularly in emerging markets: only people who have access to internet can use it. And since internet availability in rural areas, where people tend to be poorer and less educated, is rare, the demographics of those who shop online will also skew to the opposite— higher income, more educated and, as with many things new, younger. While e-commerce alone might not cover all buyers, it is still a very fast-growing distribution channel, and can (either now or in the future) influence brands' overall physical availability.

A multi-channel world

Grocery buying is part of most people's day-to-day life, with food, beverages, household goods and personal care items in constant need of replenishment. The penetration and importance of each channel varies across countries and within countries, given the large disparity between urban and rural infrastructure and services. Indeed, as modern trade expands throughout urban areas around the world, there might be more similarities in the shopping behaviours of consumers in cities in different countries, such as say Beijing and São Paulo, than between urban and rural areas within China or Brazil.

As more options become available, people add to the repertoire rather than totally substitute one for another. As a consequence, channel proliferation means people tend to shop across more channels. Table 8.1 shows the penetration of the different grocery channels from urban online panel grocery shoppers in ten emerging markets. The first observation is that *multiple channel shopping is normal* regardless of the country. This tells us that having a multi-channel presence is critical for building physical availability.

Table 8.1: Channels where urban internet-users responsible for grocery shopping (%) shopped for groceries in the last month in ten emerging markets (2014)

Country	Supermarket or hypermarket	Local or traditional market	Small/convenience store	Online
Brazil	98	90	71	39
China	98	90	88	88
India	95	95	92	58
Indonesia	90	93	95	34
Kenya	62	95	69	14
Mexico	97	89	90	28
Nigeria	66	93	82	30
Russia	96	71	83	34
South Korea	83	83	82	69
Turkey	99	90	45	40
Average	**88**	**89**	**80**	**43**

The primacy of the supermarket or hypermarket as the major location for grocery shopping throughout emerging markets becomes apparent when we look at where urban shoppers spend most of their money for groceries (Table 8.2). Differences between countries are also apparent: in Nigeria and Kenya, local and traditional markets dominate, while in India and Indonesia, more than 30% of grocery shoppers spend most of their money in local markets or small convenience stores. Finally Table 8.2 highlights that online, while more popular in South Korea and China, rarely becomes the main shopping outlet—even amongst an urban, online-savvy sample. Old (shopping) habits die hard.

Table 8.2: Channels where most money (%) is spent by urban internet users responsible for grocery shopping in ten emerging markets (2014)

Country	Supermarket or hypermarket	Local or traditional market	Small/convenience store	Online
Brazil	82	16	2	1
China	83	9	2	6
India	63	25	8	4
Indonesia	67	16	16	1
Kenya	30	61	5	1
Mexico	84	10	5	1
Nigeria	32	54	10	2
Russia	76	10	12	1
South Korea	70	11	6	10
Turkey	84	4	2	1
Average	**62**	**22**	**7**	**3**

Note: Some countries do not sum to 100% as some spending takes place in other channels.

Even with the expansion of more familiar, modern trade in emerging markets, marketers need to also negotiate both the old (traditional markets and stalls) and the new (online and mobile) channels to successfully, continuously, reach category-buying occasions.

EMERGING MARKETS: WHERE TO START?

If entering a new emerging market, start with the easy-to-manage, rising-in-importance and, most importantly, familiar options, which is modern trade (hypermarkets, supermarkets, convenience stores, large shopping centres). If a large proportion of the population lives in rural areas and they could buy your product, you have three options:

- develop relationships with nano stores, which requires developing local expertise, often educating a local sales force and making

---

adjustments in product portfolio. If you are selling chocolate in Brazil or South Africa, you want to be the one brand amongst the two or three stocked in a small store or a Spaza.

- create your own physical route to market. For example, if you are want to sell washing powder in Nigeria, you could set up a network who will educate people about the advantages of using the product while at the same time selling it. While resource intensive, this approach can be useful to grow a category that needs demonstration to get new category buyers on board; and
- look for opportunities to increase coverage and follow the trends through having a presence in e-commerce.

While achieving physical availability through modern trade channels and outlets is a must, given projected growth in urbanisation and this type of retailing, the question of the importance of nano stores and e-commerce is country and product specific. If you are in China, not selling through Alibaba means missing out on a large proportion of potential sales. If you are in India, not being in nano stores means putting the brand at a similar disadvantage.

Useful laws of shopping behaviour

Channels help us to understand broader retail structures, but buyers actually shop in retail outlets. How do people shop across retailers *and* channels? The quick answer is that choice across retailers largely mirrors the patterns of buying across brands[1]. The following are some examples:

- buyers have repertoires of retailers they visit within a category, and are rarely 100% loyal to one retailer, channel or store
- the relationship between penetration and loyalty to retailers reflects a double jeopardy pattern
- competition across retailers for shoppers follows the duplication of purchase law, whereby retailers compete in line with size of

---

1 For seminal work in the area of shopping behaviour patterns in developed and emerging markets, see Uncles & Ehrenberg (1990), Uncles & Hammond (1995) and Uncles & Kwok (2009).

the competitor. Generally, retailers share more shoppers with the more popular retailers and fewer shoppers with the less popular retailers.

- a number of structural differences between stores (format, pricing policy, location) do play a role in determining the relationship between penetration and loyalty, as well as the relative importance of specific competitors making competition between retailers a bit more complex than competition between brands. Therefore the laws can provide a framework of what is normal, which can then be used to identify deviations that help in identifying better options for building physical availability.

Shopping around

Shoppers shop around—they don't stick to one channel, let alone one retailer. Share loyalty for retail and grocery, similar to other categories, is more likely to be under 50% than not, which means typically any one store's shoppers actually shop more at other outlets.

In Figure 8.2 we see this for channels for four countries (India, China, Russia and Brazil), where surveys of internet shoppers reveal that the average channel share loyalty is around 30%, which means that 70% of grocery shopping visits occur in other channels.

Figure 8.2: Grocery retail channel share loyalty across internet-users in India, China, Russia and Brazil (2014)

In Figure 8.3 there is a similar lack of high loyalty at retailer level for buying instant coffee, which ranges from 52% for Tesco to 31% for Lidl. Spend is fragmented across supermarket retailers. Another example comes from baby-product retailers in Australia, which is a category where we might expect greater retailer loyalty as category buyers learn to trust certain outlets. But we see a similar pattern of share loyalty between 25% and 34%. People shop at multiple outlets for their baby products.

Covering multiple retailers and channels builds physical availability as shoppers rarely only shop at one outlet.

Figure 8.3: (a) Retailer share loyalty for coffee purchases in UK supermarkets (2014) and (b) baby-product purchases from Australian retailers (2013)

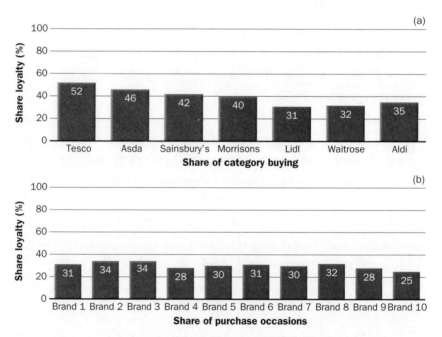

Sources: Kantar Worldwide Panel UK and Ehrenberg–Bass Institute survey

Double jeopardy in retailer choice

Channel and store choice follow the double jeopardy pattern. Channels with fewer shoppers also have shoppers who visit the store a bit less frequently (see Table 8.3 for an example from Mexico) and in Figure 8.4

we see that UK supermarkets with lower penetration also have lower repeat visitation.

Double jeopardy gives us the context to correctly interpret shopping metrics across retailers and channels. It reveals what is normal, and where retailers gain higher or lower loyalty than they should, given the size of their customer base.

Table 8.3: Double jeopardy in channel choice for in Mexico for grocery shoppers with internet access (2014)

Channel	Monthly shoppers (%)	Frequency of shopping (visits in a month)
Supermarket/hypermarket	97	6.2
Convenience	90	5.4
Local/traditional	89	5.4
Discounter	65	5.0
Online/mobile	28	4.6
Average	**74**	**5.3**

Figure 8.4: Double jeopardy in UK supermarket shopping

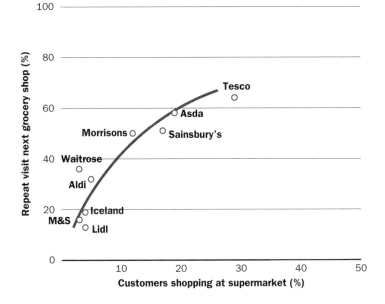

A key facet of double jeopardy, relevant for selecting channels and outlets, is that the underlying structure of the shopper bases makes low penetration outlets less attractive. Low penetration outlets have fewer shoppers, who shop there less often, and these shoppers also tend to shop at more outlets in general—so are easily reached in other more popular outlets.

Of course some major differences in format affect shopper choice, but not as much as one might imagine. Let's take South Africa, a very complex retail market with everything from hypermarkets to micro corner shops (Spaza stores). If we separate out retailers by type, we can see that the law of double jeopardy holds within each type (Table 8.4). All metrics are also closely linked to the number of stores.

Table 8.4: Double jeopardy in channel and retailer choice in South Africa for grocery shoppers (2012)

Channel	Number of stores (approx.)	Monthly shoppers (%)	Share of visits (%)	Shoppers visiting regularly (%)	Shoppers spending most money there (%)
Supermarkets					
Pick 'n' Pay	500	45	17.4	73	54
Shoprite	350	43	14.2	71	56
Checkers	275	31	10.5	70	40
Woolworths	300	14	4.7	70	16
U Save	250	2	1.1	73	28
Checkout	20	2	0.7	69	23
OK Foods	30	1	0.7	69	25
Average	**251**	**20**	**7.0**	**71**	**35**
Hypermarkets					
Pick 'n' pay	20	24	7.5	63	56
Checkers	30	14	3.7	58	48
Makro	20	3	0.5	29	28
Average	**23**	**14**	**4.0**	**50**	**44**

(continued)

Table 8.4: Double jeopardy in channel and retailer choice in South Africa for grocery shoppers (2012) (*continued*)

Channel	Number of stores (approx.)	Monthly shoppers (%)	Share of visits (%)	Shoppers visiting regularly (%)	Shoppers spending most money there (%)
Local small stores					
Spar	500	32	20.8	82	29
Spaza store	many	10	14.2	98	2
Township supermarket	many	4	3.3	90	6
Average	—	**15**	**13**	**90**	**12**

Source: National Advertising Bureau Roots survey, 2012

We see some clear deviations: Woolworths, a premium supermarket, has a lower percentage of shoppers spending most of their money there. Next, very small Spaza stores, despite high visitation, have fewer shoppers using them for their main shop. The Spaza example is partially a function of their small range but also the ever-increasing penetration of supermarkets and hypermarkets in these areas.

The real advantage of being stocked in a smaller penetration outlet, rather than a larger one, is if you can negotiate to (cheaply) give your brand greater prominence in store or to feature strongly in the outlet's above-the-line advertising activities.

The duplication of shopping law

Shoppers are not solely loyal to any one channel or retailer—so what other retail outlets do they shop at? We return to the duplication of purchase law to see how retailers compete for shoppers in today's retail environment.

Uncles and Kwok (2008, 2009) uncovered this in supermarket shopping in China, while Cohen and colleagues similarly see this for wine retailers (Cohen, Lockshin & Sharp, 2012; Lockshin & Cohen, 2011). This law also holds for grocery buying across retailers in the UK (Table 8.5). For UK supermarkets, almost every supermarket shares more

Table 8.5: Grocery retailers sharing of shoppers in the UK over a 12-week period (2012)

Stores (in penetration order)	Tesco	Asda	Sainsbury's	Morrisons	Marks & Spencer	Iceland	Aldi	Lidl	Waitrose
					Shoppers who also shopped at other stores (%)				
Tesco		48	48	38	26	26	23	25	15
Asda	67		45	44	23	28	30	26	10
Sainsbury's	70	46		39	33	23	23	25	22
Morrisons	65	54	46		29	27	29	28	14
Marks & Spencer	70	45	63	46		25	24	25	29
Iceland	74	57	46	46	27		38	34	13
Aldi	68	63	48	49	26	38		39	11
Lidl	75	56	52	49	28	36	41		18
Waitrose	71	35	74	39	50	22	18	29	
Average	**70**	**51**	**53**	**44**	**30**	**28**	**28**	**29**	**17**

Source: Ehrenberg–Bass Institute survey (unpublished), 2012

of its shoppers with Tesco (the biggest retailer) and fewer shoppers with Lidl (a hard discounter) and Waitrose (a smaller, more premium outlet). While premium supermarkets (Waitrose and Marks & Spencer) exhibit excess sharing—as do hard discounters (Aldi and Lidl)—curiously, many Marks & Spencer and Waitrose shoppers also shop at Aldi or Lidl.

We also see this amongst South African hypermarkets, as shown in Table 8.6. More shoppers at other hypermarkets *also shop* at Pick 'n' Pay, the hypermarket with more visitors, than at Makro, the hypermarket with fewer shoppers in total.

Table 8.6: Hypermarket sharing of shoppers in South Africa over a one-month period (2012)

Stores (in penetration order)	Shoppers who also shopped at other stores (%)		
	Pick 'n' Pay	Checkers	Makro
Pick 'n' Pay		23	4
Checkers	41		6
Makro	34	26	
Average	37	24	5

Source: National Advertising Bureau Roots survey, 2012

If we broaden our view beyond a single type of store—to a more complex retail environment, with hypermarkets, supermarkets and small-format stores—do we see the law still hold? The answer is broadly yes (as evident in the last row of Table 8.7, showing the average sharing figures), but with more instances of excess or deficits in sharing—related to differences in format and pricing strategy.

From Table 8.7, we can see the following:

- outlets that service lower-income areas (Spaza, Township supermarkets and Shoprite) share more shoppers than expected
- in the case of Pick 'n' Pay and Checkers, shoppers of each brand's supermarket are less likely to shop at the hypermarket (and vice versa). This is probably due to the location of stores;

Table 8.7: South African grocery retailers sharing of shoppers over a one-month period (2012)

Stores (in penetration order)	Shoppers who also shopped at other stores (%)												
	Pick 'n' Pay super	Shoprite	Spar	Check super	Pick 'n' Pay hyper	Wool-worths	Check hyper	Spaza Shop	Township super	Makro	U Save	Checkout	OK Foods
Pick 'n' Pay super		36	32	34	9†	17	10	8	3	3	1	1	1
Shoprite	38		24	21	17	6	7	18*	7	2	4	3	1
Spar	45	32		32	21	16	12	5	2	3	2	2	2
Check super	50*	28	32		22	18	6	5	2	4	2	2	2
Pick 'n' Pay hyper	17†	31	28	29		18	23*	8	4	4	2	1	1
Woolworths	54*	18†	35	40*	31*		17	4	1	6	1	1	1
Check hyper	34	22	28	14†	41*	18		3	1	6	1	2	1
Spaza Shop	37	77	16†	15†	20	5	4		21*	2	6	2	1
Township super	38	75	14†	13†	21	5	5	51*		2	4	1	1
Makro	46	27	34	36	34*	27*	26*	5	3		1	2	1
U Save	25†	64*	25	20	15	5	5	25*	6	2		8	4
Checkout	26†	63*	26	26	14	7	16	10	2	3	9		1
OK Foods	23†	31	45*	37	19	11	12	10	2	2	7	2	
Average	**36**	**42**	**28**	**26**	**22**	**13**	**12**	**13**	**5**	**3**	**3**	**2**	**1**

*>+10 percentage points difference from average
†> -10 percentage points difference from average

Source: National Advertising Bureau Roots survey 2012

rarely will a brand have a supermarket and a hypermarket in the same catchment

- shoppers at Woolworths, a premium retailer, are more likely to shop at the mainstream supermarkets (Pick 'n' Pay, Checkers) and less likely to shop at the large discounter Shoprite.

But these deviations should not distract from the main overall pattern—which is sharing in line with market share. For example, if we take Checkers supermarket, its shoppers also visit a wide variety of stores: 50% of its monthly shoppers also visit a Pick 'n' Pay supermarket, 28% also

---

HOW DO RETAILERS GROW?

The fundamental laws of buying behaviour also apply to how shoppers choose and shop from stores. What does that mean for how retailers grow? They grow by gaining many more shoppers, and most of these will be infrequent visitors to the store.

The frequency distribution of visiting or shopping from retailers shows this quite clearly. It follows the same negative binomial distribution as brand buying. In any time period, the shopper base is characterised by many light and non-shoppers and only a few shoppers visiting very frequently. We see this for large, premium and even discount grocers.

Figure 8.5: Frequency distribution of visiting or shopping in UK supermarkets

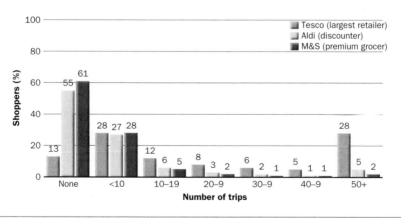

---

visit Shoprite, 32% also visit Spar, 22% also visit Pick 'n' Pay hypermarkets, 18% are also shopping at Woolworths, 6% also visit Checkers hypermarkets and 8% also visit a Spaza shop. Very few of Checkers shoppers visit Checkout, the independent supermarket, or U Save, a discount, no-frills supermarket chain, but then very few of any retailers' customer base also visit these retailers: these are small retailers.

Channel management for services: Selling versus servicing

For services, consider two aspects of presence: being present when customers buy and the everyday presence that makes it easy for customers to interact with the brand. A tangible presence has considerable value— particularly for new customers. This presence can be a retail shopfront or branch, or draw on brokers or intermediaries to act as agents. Online is, of course, also a valuable option, providing that is where customers are comfortable buying.

In the spirit of cost cutting, many banks announced they are going to cut the number of (expensive) branches, and move customers to transacting online or via ATMs. While this reduces the service costs for existing customers, who are happy not to have to visit the brand for every transaction, it makes it very difficult to sell to new customers.

A report by Bain & Co. (2013) on loyalty in the banking sector across 27 countries highlights this difference between sales and service channels. It shows that while customers conduct more transactions online or via a smartphone or tablet, it is the branch dominates as a source of new account openings. Only Germany and the Netherlands had acquisition figures from online that rivalled acquisition from branches.

Chapter 1 showed how banks cannot rely on loyalty to grow, and that acquisition is vital. Perhaps the financial services market will evolve to sell financial products online, but if a bank gets too far ahead of customer preferences, it might not be around when this evolution happens. Distinguishing between channels that sell and channels that service is important for overall management of physical availability.

While mental availability means the brand considered, physical availability is needed so that the customer will actually seek a quote. Without an easy-to-find branch, phone number or website, your mentally available brand can easily slip off the list. Potential customers often won't tell you this as they have forgotten this happened (that is the problem!).

Physical availability can also help the brand be chosen, as highlighted in the same Bain & Co report, which ranks the reasons for selecting a new bank. The list contained the usual suspects of fees, interest rates and product features. Also amongst the list of reasons ranked are some relating to physical availability including branch location, online service and ATM locations. Every country, except Belgium, had at least one of these factors in the top five (see Table 8.8).

Table 8.8: Countries with each physical availability channel ranked in top 5 reasons for selecting a new bank

Branch network	Online service	ATM locations
Argentina	Chile	Argentina
Australia	China	Chile
Canada	Denmark	China
Chile	Finland	Germany
China	France	Hong Kong
Germany	Germany	India
Hong Kong	Hong Kong	Indonesia
Indonesia	India	Italy
Japan	Indonesia	Japan
Mexico	Italy	Mexico
Netherlands	Japan	Netherlands
Russia	Netherlands	Poland
Singapore	Norway	Russia
South Korea	Poland	Singapore
Thailand	Spain	South Korea
USA	Sweden	Thailand
	UK	USA

Relevance: Is your brand buyable?

Building physical availability means creating relevant formats that buyers *can* or *want* to buy. This process is not about matching products with specific customer segments; it is about creating a product range across the category's (many) buying occasions. But balancing range with costs is important, which means narrowing down from all the possible options to the priorities. Two tasks can help here: mapping category variants to check coverage across key buying occasions, and uncovering any barriers to purchase to make the brand easier to buy.

Mapping category variants

A map of category variants can help the brand have something that is buyable for *most* of the situations that any category buyer encounters.

A product or service portfolio should be designed to meet these characteristics:

- have an option to buy in all the variants that capture substantial volume—scale is important and hence having variants that sell to a lot of people is the key
- have options to compete in areas that are growing in popularity (for example, capsules in coffee)
- have an option in any major sub-market (partitions from Chapter 3) to keep competitive as the market evolves
- avoid overweighting to any one area and over-cannibalising, particularly at the premium end where the buyer base is smaller (that is, offering three types of whitening toothpaste).

You then cover as many relevant buying situations as possible and take advantage of the future category growth areas, while avoiding over-investing in niche areas. Where one brand can't cover all options, another brand can be added to the portfolio. Channels also influence what is stockable and buyable. For example, hypermarkets require different formats from, for example, Spaza stores, where the frequency of shopping is much higher; online might offer only simple financial products, with complex ones requiring interaction with sales personnel.

Overcoming barriers to purchase

Being buyable also means dismantling any barriers to purchase, which can take a number of forms.

- *Product range*—for example, having a range of sizes from larger bulk buys to single-use packs for customers in different situations. In emerging markets, for instance, single-use sachets, while more expensive per unit, can make something an occasional treat and widen the potential market. Small formats also are easier to transport for someone who lacks a car. At the other end of the spectrum, bulk packs for household items can be very important for households with a large number of people and become more attractive when delivery is available.

- *Price-point variety*—buyers are not 100% loyal to price points but select from a range of what is available (Romaniuk & Dawes, 2005; Scriven & Ehrenberg, 2003). It is useful to have an option for when a buyer wants to splash out in a category, as well as for when someone is feeling frugal. Different occasions also demand different price levels—a bottle of wine for a dinner with my work colleagues to celebrate success as opposed to at home with friends. Finally, in emerging markets, a variety of price points gives more opportunities for those with low or irregular income to remain in the category.

- *Payment options*—wanting to buy is different from being able to buy, and flexibility in payment options is one way to remove this barrier. This can include instalment plans, credit services or mobile transfer of funds so the buyer can transact easily. For example, to grow market share in India and overcome the barrier of the initial outlay for an aspirational brand competing with many low-cost competitors, Apple has partnered with Vodafone to offer a monthly payment plan for its products including the iPhone 6 (Economic Times, 2015).

In emerging markets, structural issues about income, safe access to money and poor or inconsistent infrastructure can also impede purchase. In this case, you need to think creatively about what the brand can bring to market to smooth the path to purchase. These examples highlight ingenuity in overcoming non-product related barriers:

INCOME INSECURITY AS A BARRIER

Unpredictable incomes create mental barriers to buying non-essentials. To overcome this barrier in Vietnam, gum is available by the piece rather than the whole packet. Someone can enjoy their gum now, without worrying about paying for food and other bills come the end of the week.

TRAFFIC CONGESTION AS A BARRIER

In Chinese cities, traffic congestion is now a way of life. In Beijing, a 2011 study by UBS showed that cars go at the snail's pace of 12 kilometres per hour, while Shanghai it was 16 and Guangzhou a speedy 17 kilometres per hour! The prospect of venturing out in this traffic to go shopping is obviously quite daunting for even the most committed buyer.

Using bicycle couriers, JD and COD e-retailers can deliver goods purchased online often quicker than going to the store.

LACK OF BANKING FACILITIES AS A BARRIER

In Kenya, a key barrier to buying is lack of banking infrastructure to access money. To overcome this barrier, in the mobile airtime category in Kenya airtime is not sold as 'minutes' or 'text messages', but rather in the local currency. You can go to your local market and, via M-pesa, pay for a product in Kenyan shillings via the transfer of airtime from your phone to the vendor's phone.

This provides portability and safe storage of income, as well as easy access at retailers. It also allows family networks to transfer money to each other to balance out each individual's highs and lows with income.

Prominence: Is your brand easy to spot?

While being present is important, the brand also needs to be easily found. *Easy to buy* also means being *easy to find*. Once the brand is present in any outlet, and has buyable options, that presence is leveraged if the brand is easily found.

In retail environments, brands are surrounded by *competitive clutter* from other brands; and *situational clutter* from the environment, such as other people in stores, advertising on websites, or distractions in a mall or street making it difficult to find a retail outlet.

It is easy to underestimate the level of clutter that shoppers experience. To get some sense of this, select a similar category you don't work with and look at the brands in different shopping environments. For example, searching on taobao.com for whisky reveals 48 pages of choices, each with around 48 options. In addition to the brands in the main page, down the right hand side are another 14 images showing brands with promotions. The first page alone contains over 20 different brands to choose from. Each of those 20 different brands competes to capture the eye of the buyer, and this is more than enough for most whisky buyers to make a selection. If you go into a liquor store, how many whisky brands are available? As for duty-free outlets, all you see is a sea of whisky brands.

The nature of this clutter varies from channel to channel and from outlet to outlet, so a brand needs to be prominent enough to be easily found irrespective of the environment. For example, something on a pack that works in a store where people can pick up a product might not effectively cut through in a small two-dimensional image online.

Most outlets offer (sometimes costly) ways to make a brand more prominent, but judicious use of visual distinctive assets (see Chapter 5) can help your brand being seen and seen quickly. These assets can help build physical availability by making a brand more noticeable in its shopping environment (Romaniuk & Hartnett, 2010).

Mental availability helps your brand be the one the buyer is looking for; distinctive assets can help the buyer find the brand. Strong visual distinctive assets that cut through the competitive environment can also give the brand a chance of catching a shopper's eye in its shopping environment, even if not mentally available to the shopper at that time.

Here we must mention a dangerous yet common idea. The idea is that in order to stand out and attract attention brands should be constantly striving to look different, to employ whacky eye-catching colours, shapes and gimmicks. Some people think this is what it means to be distinctive. This idea leads to dangerous behaviours of regular pack changes, or trying not to look like you belong to your product category and, inadvertently, not looking like you. These practices slow down buyers' recognition of the brand; they make the brand harder, not easier, for people to find. Contrary to expectations, these attempts rarely actually catch the eye of shoppers, because shoppers are so astonishingly good at screening out what they are not looking for.

You want to be distinctive, not odd.

Conclusion

To build physical availability, it is useful to break it down into three components: presence—how well the brand covers places and times where buying happens; relevance—how does the brand cover the large, the partitioned and the growing areas of the market, and barriers to purchase are dealt with (where possible); and prominence—is the brand easily found by buyers?

To build presence, it is useful to remember the aim is to cover as many buying occasions as possible. In achieving this coverage, you need to keep in mind the following points:

- shoppers shop across a variety of available channels. As more channels become available, people tend to add to their channel repertoire rather than totally switch from one to another. A single-channel strategy is unlikely to get good coverage in any market.
- The availability of channels is the most important driver of shopping patterns. It's not that people are different, but availability in their location can make them behave in a particular way: change the availability, change the behaviour.
- The fundamental laws of double jeopardy and duplication of purchase (shopping) hold for channels and retailers, with some adjustment for format. Outlets with more shoppers will have those shoppers visiting more frequently and share customers more with other outlets. The shoppers who visit small outlets are rarely exclusive to that outlet.

For services, such as banking, insurance or telecommunications, invest in sales channels as well as servicing channels.

To improve a brand's relevance, design for the buying occasion, not the buyer. Buyers typically experience many different types of occasions for a category, and so ideal formats and price points will vary accordingly. This is a brand portfolio strategy rather than a segmentation strategy.

In emerging markets consider barriers to purchase, some of which might not be product related. For example, innovations in speed and safety of payment systems can dismantle a key barrier to purchase.

Finally remember that simply being present and having relevant offering is not enough; the brand needs to compete with clutter from competitors and the (often chaotic) environment. Therefore the quality of presence counts, and building prominence within the channel is also important for any brand. Visual distinctive assets can help buyers and retailers find the brand and make the most of your brand's hard-fought (often expensive) presence.

9

Online Shopping ...
Is It Different?

Magda Nenycz-Thiel and Jenni Romaniuk

E-commerce is growing. Online (and mobile) shopping can extend physical availability by reaching more people, in more places, with a wider range of options. Unsurprising, therefore, the internet is currently the fastest-growing distribution channel—now selling everything from basic grocery needs through to displaying cars and houses. But expansion online means playing in a different competitive field, and the strengths offline might not translate into the online environment. When should a brand prioritise online as a channel? What changes does physical availability in an online channel bring? How can you best use your online presence? We present research on how online environment is affecting how buyers shop and choose, and show how this should affect your online channel decisions.

Growth in e-commerce

The trend in e-commerce around the world is clear: online and mobile sales are on the rise. The number of online shoppers overall in the USA is predicted to surpass 200 million, or over 60% of US households, in 2015 (Statista, 2015). In the UK, online retail sales are predicted to reach £52.25 billion in 2015 (Moth, 2015).

But the real growth in this space is in emerging markets. The online and mobile worlds can make products available to many who otherwise could not be reached through bricks-and-mortar stores. It is predicted that, by 2020, China's e-commerce market will be larger than the ones of the USA, the UK, Japan, Germany and France combined (KPMG, 2014). Fuelling this growth is the strong presence of e-commerce platforms, like Tmall. While Alibaba's Tmall reaches many more shoppers than any physical retailer, Tmall is just one of many Chinese e-commerce companies, such as Jindong, Amazon China, Dangdang, 51buy, Yihaodian and Suning. These companies are all working to increase their footprint in the Chinese retail market. China is just one example; amazing innovations are taking place in other countries, like Ocado's 'virtual shopping' walls that allow purchases by mobile phones scanning barcodes in the Seoul underground (Mccormick, 2011), or the most sophisticated mobile payment system in the developing world, M-Pesa, in Kenya and Tanzania.

Online shopping has the potential to remove geographical boundaries and offers innovative ways of making payments, same-day or convenient deliveries and, of course, greater choice. The business innovations in the digital space also challenge the conventional definitions of a *retailer* and the parts of the business for which it is responsible.

JUMIA—WHERE THE IMPOSSIBLE IS POSSIBLE

Lack of infrastructure is a key problem in securing distribution in emerging markets. A dearth of useful distribution, transportation and storage networks, coupled with inconsistent essential services such as power and water, provide challenges to building physical availability.

Nigeria is an excellent example of a country where potential is stifled by infrastructure shortfalls.

In the face of this challenge, two young graduates of the Paris Business School—Jeremy Hodara and Sacha Poignonnec—created an Amazon-like retail channel, Jumia, where consumers can buy anything, pay for their purchases in a variety of ways and have their goods delivered the day after the order was made.

To succeed, Jumia not only had to offer the conventional benefits of an online store (range, quick delivery, payment options) but also develop the infrastructure it needed to operate. Jumia has its own delivery systems, to compensate for North Africa's poor mail services. To overcome the lack of banking infrastructure, Jumia developed its own payment systems to cater to the wide variety of needs in terms of online payment risk, income levels and availability of payment cards. Jumia is now present in Nigeria, Egypt, Morocco, Kenya and Côte d'Ivoire.

Access to a shopper world with no boundaries?

Hypothetically, an online channel does not suffer the constraints of a physical location, offering buyers an option to buy in situations when hard infrastructure is not in place. And part of the value proposition that online shopping offers is the lack of bricks-and-mortar store set-up costs. But, in reality, if buyers don't come to you, you need to go to them. Selling products still requires delivery logistics, which means that location, or in this case, the ability to deliver cost-effectively and efficiently to the customer, still matters, even online.

In developed markets, it's hard to find locations where the logistics would be a real issue; even small villages in Germany, the UK or the USA get regular service from delivery companies. Online shopping overcomes the lack of choice and higher prices that often plague regional and rural communities (Bell, 2014). But in emerging markets, the rural areas are rarely reachable by cost-effective logistics and these places also suffer from poor internet coverage. While online could be a solution in rural areas, it is the urban parts of emerging markets where e-commerce is booming.

That said, the sheer number of people living in rural locations and the rise in internet users is being recognised by the likes of Alibaba, who are making service to shoppers in rural areas a strategic priority (Sugawara, 2014). Packaged goods companies such as Unilever are looking at technologies such as 3-D printers to overcome supply chain issues but these solutions still require strong, continuous sources of energy to run, something many rural communities lack (Joseph, 2015).

Do you need an online presence?

When deciding whether to add online to your channel mix, first consider how many shopping occasions for the category would you miss (now and in the near future) if the brand is not available online, now, and also the investment in money, time and strategic capabilities needed to do online well. This involves taking into consideration two interlocking factors: the e-commerce evolution of the country or region *and* the category you are operating in.

First, countries differ immensely in e-commerce maturity. In China e-commerce is a more mature, large and important channel for an increasing number of categories; the retailers are large and concentrated; and logistics are already well set up, with efficient delivery systems. To gain market share in China, e-commerce needs to be a major consideration, as failure to operate in this space likely means many missed shopping occasions. E-commerce can also be an opportunity, and help to avoid the complexities of setting up a physical retail location. But in India, e-commerce is still in its infancy, and so challenges such as taxation, cost effectively shipping many small packages, payment security and consumer acceptance need to be considered before entry.

Next, some categories are better for the online world than others. For example, in China in 2013, more than 80% of online shoppers bought apparel and accessories online in the previous three months compared to about 55% for beverage and packaged foods and 30% for baby products (Nielsen, 2014). If you are selling apparel, being online in China is important to cover shopping occasions, but if you are selling chocolate or soft drinks, securing presence in physical channels is a greater priority.

If you decide online is a viable or necessary option, a good way to start is by making your portfolio partially available online; and focus first on products or services that meet these characteristics:

- people feel comfortable buying the product or service online—for example, people might be comfortable buying car insurance online, because it is a simple transaction, but life insurance might be best sold via a face-to-face or phone channel. Similarly there might be resistance to buying products with shorter-term expiry dates (such as milk or yoghurt) but longer-life dairy products might be perfectly acceptable.
- the products or services offer a direct consumer benefit for purchasing online—for example, home delivery means bulky, large-volume products that have routinised consumption (dog food, nappies, toilet paper) are likely to be attractive online purchases.

What differences does the online channel bring?

Let's start with *who* shops online. The research across a number of markets shows that online shoppers are generally younger, with have higher education and income levels (Nielsen, 2015). This simply reflects the typical heavy internet access skews; particularly when penetration is not yet close to saturation point, those online more are more likely to shop online.

Shopping online also often includes a delivery service, which appeals to those who lack mobility—carless, new families and older people (but only those who are online!). More recently, advances in 'click-and-collect' options widen the base of those willing and able to shop online by removing the need to be at home at a specific delivery time.

Research into online grocery buying shows that online buyers of any supermarket retailer are mostly existing buyers of that same offline supermarket retailer (around 66% overlap) (Dawes & Nenycz-Thiel, 2014; Melis et al., in press). Tesco offline shoppers are also likely to be Tesco's online shoppers, so, unsurprisingly, they take at least some of the shopping habits from in-store to the online space!

There are several structural ways the online environment differs from offline. A key one is the searchable online brand list, whereby all brands are present. In-store, stock-outs can lead to some brands being unavailable, and the buyer needing to find an immediate substitute. A second difference is the function of saveable shopping lists helps remind people of the products or brands they last bought. Some online retailers even add a 'have you forgotten' system before check out to remind people of categories and brands bought previously but not on this occasion.

These structural differences all serve to make it easy to buy brands previously bought when shopping online, which suggest loyalty to the most preferred brand will be higher for online shoppers. If this is the case, then something has to be lower—and most likely this higher loyalty will be at the expense of impulse, promotional or 'just buy that brand because I can't find the one I want' brand purchases. Buyers might still have a repertoire, but it will be more stable over time.

Another way online differs from offline is that delivery makes it easier to stockpile favourite brands (for example, when on special). This might also lead to higher loyalty online.

How does shopping online influence loyalty?

First, let's test for the law of double jeopardy, which is that small brands are penalised twice, with (many) fewer buyers who are (slightly) less loyal. Arguably within an e-retailer's shopping environment, physical availability evens out across brands, as bigger brands do not command the same shelf space advantage as they do typically in-store—a small brand has similar real estate to a large brand. We might not see the same small brand disadvantage in the online environment, and double jeopardy might not occur.

Here we look at a couple of different examples to see if the double jeopardy law holds.

Table 9.1 shows buying of a normal grocery category online, compared to its purchases offline. We see that the law of double jeopardy holds for toothpaste purchasing in the online environment as well as offline—even the brand ranks are the same. In both the offline and online shopper worlds, the main difference between competing brands is how many people buy them, while loyalty varies much less and in line with brand penetration.

Table 9.1: Double jeopardy for toothpaste buying online and offline in the UK (2014)

Brand (rank order)	Offline sales (91% of total sales)		Online sales (9% of total sales)	
	Penetration over a year (%)	Average purchase frequency	Penetration over a year (%)	Average purchase frequency
Colgate	71	3.1	63	2.4
Aquafresh	23	2.1	27	2.3
Oral B	20	2.1	15	1.8
Sensodyne	15	2.4	12	2.1
Macleans	10	1.7	6	2.0
Arm+Hammer	9	1.9	4	1.8
Tesco Steps	1	1.6	3	1.8
Average	**21**	**2.1**	**18**	**2.0**

Source: Kantar Worldwide Panel UK

Yes there are some brands that have a higher penetration online (Aquafresh, Tesco Steps), but this does not change their rank order. This also shows us it is not just about physical availability but that mental availability also contributes a great deal to the advantages of big brands. Small brands need to claw back this advantage when competing online.

Next let's consider e-commerce sites and shopper visiting behaviour online. In this case monthly Nielsen website visitation figures for e-retailers shows a clear double jeopardy pattern (Table 9.2). Amazon.com has many more visitors that visit slightly more often and stay for longer each time on the site. Sites with fewer visitors are also visited less often by their shoppers, and these shoppers spend less time on the site. Even the wholesale shopping clubs, Costco and Sam's Club, do not deviate substantively from this pattern.

Table 9.2: Double jeopardy in e-commerce sites (2014)

Site	Active reach (%)	Sessions per person	Time per person (hh:mm:ss)
Amazon	39.0	8.4	0:54:43
Walmart Stores	22.4	4.5	0:23:42
Target	13.3	3.1	0:15:32
Overstock.com	5.0	2.1	0:09:31
Staples	4.3	2.9	0:12:28
AliExpress	4.2	2.3	0:08:29
Costco	3.9	2.4	0:10:50
Sam's Club	3.8	2.4	0:10:40
Average	**12.0**	**3.5**	**0:18:14**

Source: Nielsen online panel

As the final example, we turn to fashion retail. This category has substantive growth in online sales but—unlike, say, books or music—has retained a strong bricks and mortar presence. In Figure 9.1, we see double jeopardy in both bricks and mortar and online stores, and for visits as well as purchases. Smaller retailers have fewer visitors and purchasers who devote less of their share of visits and purchases to them. Essentially the online shopper stage looks very similar to the bricks-and-mortar world, just with a different set of actors.

While loyalty patterns to stores and brands online look familiar, what about loyalty levels? Are people more loyal to brands when they shop online? Table 9.3 shows five different packaged goods categories from the Kantar Worldpanel in the UK in 2013 and 2014, across the same set of brands sold in both environments. In all categories, loyalty to brands is

Figure 9.1: Double jeopardy in fashion for visits and purchases in Singapore (2014)

Table 9.3: Average share of category requirements online and offline in the UK (2013–14)

Category	Share loyalty (2013)		Share loyalty (2014)	
	Offline (%)	Online (%)	Offline (%)	Online (%)
Dog food	21	33	20	34
Instant coffee	31	48	31	49
Nappies	28	42	33	41
Fabric	38	50	37	50
Toothpaste	35	43	37	41
Average	**31**	**43**	**32**	**43**

Source: Kantar Worldwide Panel UK

consistently higher online than offline. For example, in 2013, share loyalty to dog food offline is 21% while online it rises to 33%. The 2014 figures mirror this pattern.

While past research from 2010 found slightly higher loyalty online than offline, averaging 2.4% (Dawes & Nenycz-Thiel, 2014), this more recent data suggests an increasing disparity in loyalty levels. But we must put these loyalty figures in context: loyalty levels are still a long way from 100%, even though the online shopping conditions are conducive for them to be.

Why is loyalty higher online? We tested to see if stockpiling was an explanation but there is little evidence that people buy in higher quantities online. The difference in packs per occasion between buying offline and online is typically negligible (only three out of 100 cases had more than one pack sold online).

One of the reasons for the higher loyalty could be the availability of saveable shopping lists or favourites. Online platforms remember previous purchases and make recommendations based on these. Even if this is an influence, repertoire buying is still the norm as share loyalty figures are still typically below 50% online.

A third explanation is that as online shopping becomes a more frequent behaviour, more categories will have a greater proportion of light category buyers buying online. When people start online shopping, frequently bought categories are on the list first as need for these categories is more likely to coincide with the online shopping occasion (indeed a need for say, dog food or nappies, might drive the timing of the online shop). But these people are still shopping offline as well. As online shopping occurs more frequently, shopping timing can also coincide with categories bought less frequently, and so the number of categories that person buys online expands. As a greater proportion of light category buyers buy a brand online, their relative infrequency of buying makes higher share loyalty likely.

We looked very carefully, but could not see any consistent advantages for small brands online. If anything, the higher loyalty online makes it more challenging for small brands to enter buyer repertoires in this shopping environment. Even with a more levelled physical availability playing field, differences in mental availability mean big brands still have many advantages online.

And for retailers?

Since the online space offers shoppers an additional channel and more retail brands to choose from, and all of this (almost) independent of location, multi-channel shopping also affects shopper loyalty to retailers. Shoppers do not substitute an offline store with an online option but rather expand their store repertoires and buy from more retailers, in more channels (Dawes & Nenycz-Thiel, 2014; Melis et al., in pess).

Over time, after the initial plunge into online grocery shopping, we see highlighted competition between online channels. This shows that, once having entered the online world and bought at one online retailer (most likely the one which was their main chain offline), shoppers easily enter other online stores. This means that online buying can negatively affect loyalty to *retailers*.

Still, the majority of shoppers purchase a product in person, even if they found it, read reviews or compared prices online. We see this in a recent study we conducted into the pre-purchase shopping behaviour for 150 first-time buyers of mobile phones in India. There were two groups of first-time buyers: those buying a feature phone for the first time, and those upgrading to their first smartphone.

We see no difference in the length of time from starting to think about the category to making a purchase—around one month for 70% of both types of new category buyers. Shopping outlets are also similar— around 95% researched the produce online (the sample group were active internet active users and researching an electronic product), while around 70% visited bricks-and-mortar stores. But, while both types of new category buyers visited the same number of online stores (around four), feature phone new buyers visited more bricks-and-mortar stores (around four) than smartphone new category buyers (only one or two stores). This means being easy to find in a physical presence is even more important to reach new smartphone buyers, who visit fewer stores during the purchase process.

Shopping is quick—online too

Finally, with all the available search options and possibilities to customise how we buy, how does online shopping behaviour compare to offline, in terms of time spent actually shopping? The answer is, that similar to offline, shopper behaviour online is quick, with more than half of purchases made in 13 seconds (Anesbury et al., 2014).

For both retailers and manufacturers, these findings highlight the (continued) importance of the in-store experience and prominence—whether that be physical or digital. If the desired product is not easily (quickly) available and recognisable, it won't enter the shopper's basket. And since shoppers save their baskets for later, not being chosen when they are formed means a significant lost opportunity. It's up to the retailers to create the environment for easy shopping and for manufacturers to make their brands easy to find—located well and visually distinctive—within this environment.

Conclusion

E-commerce space is dynamic. Things change quickly and staying on top of the developments in your category and market is crucial. We leave you with some key points for competing for online shoppers, based on what we know today.

Online is not a must for every category or country—this decision depends on the online maturity of the market you operate in and your category. It has to be profitable and should not harm your offline business.

Shoppers are shoppers, online or off—shoppers of your online stores are largely category buyers with online access. If you have an offline presence as well, expect quite a bit of overlap, and make the transition easy and familiar. If you only sell online, expect to still compete with offline channels. But expect the laws of marketing, such as double jeopardy, to still apply.

Plan the online portfolio carefully—any retail space is expensive, including online. Make the most of it by cherry-picking from your portfolio for the online environment. Choose categories and stock-keeping units (SKUs: large sizes, for example) that offer real convenience to shoppers; avoid options that might face resistance.

Plan for repertoire buying—it's easy to imagine a world where everyone becomes solely loyal to the brand of their dream, but we know that, despite the many opportunities for people to be solely loyal, the natural tendency is towards repertoire buying. Plan for this: for example, retailers, rather than recommending just one brand for a category not bought that shopping trip, could offer the shopper the last three brands he or she bought to choose from.

All (online) presence is not equal—online shopping is fast, which means that investing in good-quality presence is critical. If you do pay more for this, then prioritise your best sellers. Creating distinctive assets that can work on a cluttered online page helps draw attention to the brand.

Gaining penetration online is going to be more difficult than offline—the trend for online grocery shopping is towards more loyalty, which means fewer slots in buyers' repertoires. This means it will be harder to break through and get bought for the first time online. This also has implications for new introductions, and suggests they are better off focusing marketing efforts offline than online when trying to break into buyer repertoires.

Mental availability matters, even online—strong physical availability online is only part of the battle; you also need to invest in out-of-store activities to raise the mental availability of the brand, and make it one of the ones the buyer looks for. This may help overcome the tendency to loyalty online, and help the brand break into buyers' repertoires. Investing in more channels is not an excuse to cut back on advertising.

Make it easy to shop—this applies to offline and online environments but online it is much easier *not* close the sale. We rarely leave the supermarket because of some minor frustration about not being able to find exactly what we wanted or the price being higher than we expected, but it is easy to abandon a shopping basket online and move to a different online store.

10

New Brands and Acquiring New Buyers

Jenni Romaniuk and Byron Sharp

N ew brand launches are exciting but risky endeavours. In this chapter we highlight some assumptions that adversely affect new launch marketing strategy, unwittingly lessening the chances of success. We reveal how the mental structures of new brand buyers look like light brand buyers, rather than someone who recently underwent a radical conversion to buy the brand. And we discuss what this means for advertising to grow penetration.

To build penetration we need to recruit new 'brains' to brands—you can think of this as the zombie strategy. To survive and grow, the brand needs to go out and reach (gobble up) as many new brains as possible. We explain how to use mental and physical availability to recruit these very important buyers, and the implications for media planning.

We show how recruiting heavy category buyers is a necessary but not sufficient condition for success, and reveal how to discover the *normal* cannibalisation a new brand will generate if you launch an additional brand or variant into your category.

A special occasion: The birth of a new brand

The launch of a new brand is full of promise and opportunity. Nothing else quite galvanises the marketing department, and careers have blossomed (and crashed) based on the performance of a new launch. The *promise* of what the launch might be makes it easier to ask for money, and spend a disproportionate amount of time and resources to trying to make this new launch successful. Secret new teams are formed, with code names worthy of a James Bond movie. But with this investment come great, often unfulfilled, expectations.

Figure 10.1: The birth of a new brand is an exciting event

> **Birth notice: Bingo! Plc**
>
> After a long labour of feasibility studies and fighting over budgets, the marketing department of Bingo! Plc are delighted to announce the birth of new brand 'Bango' into the Upper Volta toothpick market on December 3 2015, weighing between 50 and 200 in pack size.
>
> The proud parents hope that Bango will attract a substantial, loyal buyer base and find its own profitable place in a cluttered, competitive category.

New launches can be a company's first entry into the category or can add to the portfolio. Additions to the portfolio can be separate brands or variants that share a similar name. Variants can gain from a head start in building both physical and mental availability but risk excess cannibalisation and often fail to win incremental sales or profits.

The 'arduous' path to first purchase

The cruel reality is that, when a new brand enters a category, most category buyers just continue buying the brands they always have. Why is this? The traditional (exaggerated) explanation is that a buyer needs to be convinced of some benefit to change from their existing repertoire: that they need a reason or an intense emotional desire. The textbook recommendation is for a new brand to have a value proposition that exceeds existing brands, that it must be very differentiated, and that the advertising very persuasive. If people don't buy a new brand, it's thought to be because it failed to be worthy or convincing enough—or both.

But let's come down to earth and look at markets full of busy consumers, who are naturally loyal and managing to make their category purchases without the new launch brand. Low brand knowledge, even for the buyers of an existing brand, is the norm. The distribution of brand associations usually follows a Pareto share pattern, similar to sales, of 20:50, with the top 20% holding around half the category purchasers' total knowledge of the brand, with the remaining 80% holding the other half of the brand's knowledge (Romaniuk & Sharp, 2003). What this means is that many existing customers know very little about existing brands, and non-brand buyers know even less.

Let's take a relatively new brand, Coke Zero, and compare the amount of knowledge across three buyer groups: very light and non-buyers; recent new buyers who bought the brand for the first time in the last three months; and longer-term buyers who have been buying the brand for more than three months.

We see (Figure 10.2) that in terms of brand knowledge, recent new buyers sit somewhere in between very light and non-buyers and longer-term buyers. These recent buyers know something about the brand, but six in ten of new buyers don't know very much, with fewer than three brand associations (out of a possible 18). This is not unusual: of longer-term

Figure 10.2 Recent new buyer brand associations for Coke Zero

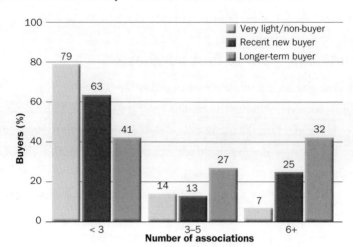

Coke Zero buyers, *four in ten buyers also know very little about the brand.* It is quite normal for a brand to have the majority of its buyers with only a few accessible mental structures; recent new buyers skew even more to having little accessible brand knowledge.

Brands are therefore fairly 'new' (unknown) to most category buyers, whether they are long established or new launches. For many buyers, brands that were launched years ago are still unknown to them. This tells us that perhaps the process for a new brand attracting a new buyer is not that different from an existing brand attracting a new buyer. In both cases, it is a question of how much mental availability you need to build for someone to buy you for the first time.

To answer this question, we first look at buying behaviour: the metrics of new launches, and the buying patterns of buyers of a newly launched brand. Then we move onto the underlying mental structures of new brand buyers and how you can build that army of new brains for the brand.

New brands grow in the same way as existing brands

Research examining new launches shows that the metrics of new brands settle down remarkably quickly to be very similar to existing brands of similar share (Ehrenberg & Goodhardt, 2001; Wright and Sharp, 2001).

New brands, even in emerging markets, grow more via penetration than improvement in loyalty metrics. As an example, Table 10.1 shows a toothpaste brand launched in China—year-on-year penetration grew considerably more than either loyalty metric.

Table 10.1 The growth of a new toothpaste brand in China

Year	Value share (%) and change (%)	Penetration (%) and change (%)	Purchase frequency (%) and change (%)	Share loyalty and change (%)
1	0.002	0.02	0.9	10
2	0.25 (+1200)	0.4 (+1900)	1.1 (+22)	10 (+0)
3	1 (+292)	1 (+150)	1.4 (+27)	13 (+30)

New launches in any market are initially (very) small brands with few customers. Unsurprisingly then, they need to recruit new customers to grow, yet it's not uncommon for new launch marketing plans to focus on winning the loyalty of a few rather than reaching the masses.

A common but fanciful idea is that it's best to win over a few opinion leaders in the hope they become advocates for the brand. The enormous risks associated with this sort of strategy are too often glossed over. Marketing consultants sell secret techniques to identify a special group of consumers whom the new brand is supposed to be targeting. The names change, but the idea is old: golden households, innovators, super consumers, brand influencers. All very entertaining, and good business for the consultants, but you needn't part with your money as it's actually very easy to predict which buyers are the most likely to buy your new brand first, and who you need to recruit to grow the new launch.

Who buys first?

Heavy category buyers look like tempting targets and they do tend to be a sizeable portion of a new brand's initial buyers. They notice and buy the brand sooner than other category buyers, because these buyers are simply in the market more often. The timing of their buying is more likely to overlap with when the new launch is making a splash.

Statistically, a heavy category buyer is more likely to buy a new brand than a light category buyer (Taylor, 1977)—but what happens after that? Such heavy category buyers, who buy the category a lot, could also easily become super loyal to the brand; they certainly make enough category purchases to be able to do so. Unfortunately, the vast majority of heavy category buyers become *light buyers of the new launch*, maintaining a large number of other brands in their repertoire. The new launch becomes part of the entourage, rather than the star of the repertoire.

Remember a natural characteristic of heavy category buyers is that they buy more brands. This is illustrated in Figure 10.3, for soft drinks in Turkey, Nigeria and Mexico. Those buying soft drinks less than once a month only bought two or three brands, while those buying more frequently, at least once a day, bought between six and seven brands.

As the new launch slips into their repertoires usually quite a long way down, the heavy category buyers do not typically end up being of substantial value *per customer* to the new launch. This means one should be cautious about paying a great deal to acquire heavy category buyers.

Figure 10.3 The relationship between frequency of buying and number of brands bought for soft drinks in Turkey, Nigeria and Mexico (2014)

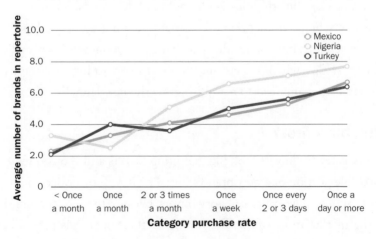

New (and small) brands have a customer base skewed to heavier category buyers; to grow, they have to correct this skew by recruiting lighter category buyers—as this is what the customer base of large, established brands looks like. Put simply, recruiting heavy category buyers is not enough—it's impossible to grow without extending the brand's footprint out so that it recruits an awful lot of light category buyers.

Hang around long enough to reach light and medium category buyers

Existing brands have many light brand buyers who buy it over a longer time frame: many of these are also light category buyers. To grow, new launches have to (eventually) attract these lighter category buyers. This can only happen if the brand continues to advertise beyond the initial launch period, and builds mental availability amongst those who are less frequently in the market for the category.

What about loyalty?

What of the role of loyalty in the ongoing success of a new brand? New launches have systematically lower loyalty when compared to existing brands of similar market share (Trinh, Romaniuk & Tanusondjaja, 2015). This lower loyalty is not a sign of impeding failure and is seldom due to people trialling and then rejecting the brand (all brands are rejected a little but not much). Rejection by first-time buyers is seldom a reason for failure today, because most marketers conduct decent tests beforehand to prevent such disasters. The main reason for this slightly lower loyalty is that new brands temporarily buy physical and mental availability, and even give price discounts, all of which results in some purchases that fail to be repeated when this support for the brand disappears (that is, when it gets a bit harder to buy for some people).

Singh and colleagues (2012) recently examined fairly successful brand extensions—that is, those that secured more than 0.5% market share and stayed in the market for at least a couple of years. They found a group of these brands that within a year started to decline. In other words, they did rather well at winning share for two or three quarters but then faltered. Interestingly, while the penetration and purchase-frequency metrics for these particular brands always looked about normal, their quarter-to-quarter repeat rates were low. This fits with a brand attracting sales through temporary in-store displays and discounts, and bursts of advertising.

Perhaps the lesson here is *start as you mean to go forward*. Planning a special launch, with a burst of enticements, sounds like the right sort of thing to build mental and physical availability for something new. But if the schedule is heavy on temporary inducements and then followed by a trough, this is unlikely to build the mental and physical availability necessary to sustain the brand's share.

BASES, Nielsen's sales forecasting consultancy, once pointed out that Apple's launch of the iPod featured a steady and increasing media spend, each quarter more than the previous one. Yes, we saw it at launch, but we also saw it over the longer term as well. It didn't just make an entrance and fade away.

So why do many new launches fail? Typically they fail to gain *both* penetration and loyalty. This is because they fail to do the hard work to build the necessary mental and physical availability. One of the reasons for this is, in the thrill of the new launch, marketers overestimate the excitement their new brand might generate. A few excited new buyers won't replace the investment that builds widespread mental and physical availability[1]. They bank on any excitement and word of mouth doing too much of the work. It would take astonishing amount of excitement to make up for even small shortfalls in mental and physical availability.

Launches usually feature an intense burst of activity, followed by silence until more budget is available. Per dollar spend this delivers low reach; it also means that many future category purchases will not have been preceded by recent ad exposure.

---

1   Even if these excited buyers are super-influentials, they only will account for a small amount of word of mouth. See Watts and Dodds (2007) for more on word-of-mouth diffusion.

A two-stage launch strategy

Don't be dismayed at lower-than-expected loyalty figures for a new launch (compared to a similarly sized existing brand) and don't use this as a reason to cut investment. Instead, think about a new launch in two stages.

Stage 1: Attract enough initial sales to secure and build the brand's physical distribution. Remember, you don't need to target heavy category buyers specifically—their natural buying patterns mean that they will find you! Choose wide-reach activities, but realise that it is heavier category buyers who are more likely to initially respond. So that you have funds for stage 2, minimise frequency, but make sure every exposure counts and advertised messages resonate with heavy category buyers.

Stage 2: Be continually 'on air' to reach medium and light category buyers as they enter their buying cycles. Make sure your messages are relevant to medium and light category buyers, which might mean a change from initial launch messaging.

CANNIBALISATION: HOW MUCH IS TOO MUCH?

One of the major concerns on second brand or variant launches is cannibalisation—where the new launch 'steals' sales from an existing brand from the same company. Some level of cannibalisation is normal but how much is too much?

The duplication of purchase law (Chapter 3) gives a benchmark for how much cannibalisation to expect. It shows how much the overlap between your two brands' customer bases should be. Aim to avoid any more overlap than this benchmark. Sometimes you might accept a higher rate than this, but this is a strategic choice to steal your own sales rather than let a competitor steal them from you. The new brand is simply to block a competitive launch.

How to avoid excessive cannibalisation? The traditional strategy is to target the brand towards a different type of buyer but this may hamper the chance of a new brand being successful. Brands (which survive their launch) end up selling to much the same sort of customers as their rivals. Dreaming of positioning the new brand so that it does not sell to the

---

same sort of people who buy your existing brand is largely, well, wishful thinking—and may backfire by limiting the brand's sales.

Excess sharing can be avoided or rectified in these ways:

- *building physical availability*—widening distribution of the smaller brand so that it is not just overlapping with the existing brand
- *building mental availability*—establishing a propensity to think of the new launch, separate from the propensity to think of any parent brand, so it competes mentally in line with other brands (not owned by the same company).

These strategies are likely to enhance overall sales, as well as prevent excess stealing from the original brand.

Priority mental structures for a new brand (buyer)

What might you need to know before you buy a brand for the first time? It's a useful management exercise to consider what memories are essential for potential buyers to hold (in your categories). The memories that, if absent, make it unlikely that they will buy your brand. Contrary to marketing textbook logic, these are not beliefs concerning the brand's superiority or its difference from other brands.

The first, most essential memories to build are simply what this brand is and what it looks like (so it can be found). Often this is a case of saying 'we are an(other) accounting service' or 'we are an(other) soft drink'—and this is our name, this is what we look like, this is where and how you can buy us. If you don't get these facts into people's memories then you have very little chance of being bought.

It should be obvious, yet a surprising amount of new brand marketing communication does a very poor job of doing this, all too often because the marketing plan focused on teaching (part of) the market what was different about the brand. People aren't looking for difference: they are looking to understand the brand, looking for signals as to where it would be useful to store the brand in their memory.

TIP: BORROW MEMORIES

A brand that is new to a market, even if it is famous overseas, suffers from a lack of mental availability. Its lack of physical availability and sales mean that few consumers see other consumers using the brand, or hear them mention it—so no groundswell base supports your own marketing activities. A lack of distinctive assets means branding relies on the name, which makes quickly building mental availability difficult. This all sounds daunting, and it is, but it's not impossible to overcome.

One tip is to start by working with existing cultural memory structures. Know how potential buyers already see the category and brands within it. Advertising must also work with the collective knowledge, symbolism, and mores of the particular market (the local culture). And look out for archetypes, colours, symbols that have immediate communication power to associate your brand with the category. These can visually support the category entry points (CEPs) you are developing to build mental availability. This strategy needs to be coupled with a distinctive asset palette (see Chapter 5). The aim is to attach new brand memories to established category memories.

Snack-food marketer Mars had a problem in India that chocolate is an after-meal treat, but not something that could be taken to work as a snack. Its Snickers chocolate bar suffered from a lack of mental linkage to these very important consumption situations. By linking Snickers to *tiffin*, which in India refers to light, between-meal snacks and to the silver tins used to transport them, Mars was able to borrow these between-meal memory structures and visual images of Snickers in the silver tins and attach the brand to this common potential consumption occasion (for an advertising example, see <https://www.youtube.com/watch?v=ouwr2HeTjGI>).

Buying a brand for the first time doesn't require a major conversion, just a little salience. Think of new brand buyers as lighter users, rather than converted disciples (Trinh, Romaniuk & Tanusondjaja, 2015). This makes sense: remember, most of your buyers are like this. New recruits do not suddenly leap to the top of the attitude or image charts—they just have enough useful mental structures and sufficient physical availability to get them over the line to be able to be bought when a buying occasion presents itself.

After establishing links to the category, the next important step is to develop the depth of mental availability amongst category buyers, and have the brand compete as a viable option in different buying situations. To build to this, the new brand, like any other, needs to form links to category entry points (CEPs). Like any other brand, in the long run, the more links to more CEPs the better placed the brand will be. But a new brand is usually in a race to generate initial sales, necessary to hold and win more physical availability. This makes some memories more important to lay down first.

Prioritise common CEPs—this is where the volume is

CEPs vary in how often they are relevant for buyers in a category. Some CEPs have widespread relevance, while others are rarely used. Commonly encountered CEPs are more valuable for a brand, as they create more opportunities where the brand *could* be salient. For example, comparing the relevance of CEPs for whisky, *something to help me relax* is more common than for *a special gift*. Signalling the brand is useful in a gifting or a treat context is useful but, as it rarely comes up, it might not be the best starting point for the brand as strong links to this CEP will only help in these (rare) occasions.

A commonly used CEP has more brands competing for retrieval (Romaniuk & Gaillard, 2007). This means excellent branding is needed to avoid confusion or misattribution to competitor brands already embedded in buyers' memories. Creativity helps your brand gain cut-through but without quality branding any advertising budget is quickly wasted.

Prioritise branding quality across all touch-points

The brand anchors the advertised message in the right place in buyer memory. Advertising exposure can't build mental availability if the viewer can't correctly identify the advertised brand. Broadly speaking, two types of branding tactics exist:

- directly by showing or saying the brand name
- indirectly via distinctive assets (covered in Chapter 5).

Being new to the category, a new launch won't have distinctive assets to use, as these take time and repeat exposure to build. New launches can set the goal of building distinctive assets, and incorporate such elements into creative executions. But launch campaigns need to have crystal-clear execution of the brand name, both for effective advertising and to lay the groundwork for building distinctive assets for the future.

Remember that the first buyers of a new launch are likely to be heavy category buyers who use many brands and so notice the advertising of these brands. These buyers could easily think of and buy many other brands if the advertisement reminds them only of the category (and not the new brand). Strong branding requires using smart execution tactics to make the brand a prominent and noticeable part of the advertisement (or indeed any other marketing activity).

The general rule is that your brand should be obvious to everyone, including those who have little or no knowledge about the brand or who are paying very little attention when they are viewing or listening to the advertisement—or both.

In practice this means branding that:

- is early
- is visually frequent
- is spaced out within the advertisement (not all bunched up at the end)
- has both visual and audio components where possible.

(See Romaniuk, 2009, for more evidence and background to effective television or brand placement execution tactics.)

But what about more unusual CEPs—won't they be easier to win?

The illusory Holy Grail is where the new launch finds one CEP it can own (for example, to take to a graduation party; when celebrating your sixtieth wedding anniversary). This search for a unique CEP is risky for two reasons:

- a CEP that is rarely used by rivals is usually also less commonly used by category buyers. The fewer occurrences where the brand might be retrieved makes it harder to achieve the volume of sales needed in a short period of time.
- these less common CEPs are usually less relevant to light category buyers, who have more general category needs. Uncommon CEPs are more likely to be used, on the rare occasion they are relevant, by heavy category buyers. Therefore while an uncommon CEP might help initially gaining interest from heavy category buyers, unless framed very carefully, ongoing promotion of that same message will hamper the recruitment of lighter category buyers. This is why new launch messages should be tested on both heavy and light category buyers.

Selecting an uncommon or unique CEP might be a route into a market, but it means that the new launch is left mentally competing on rare occasions for a few heavy category buyers. This is not a recipe for large sales volumes. Remember from Chapter 4 that a brand that is big will be considered applicable to all of the major CEPs in the category.

Again, why not start as you mean to go on!

Rejection check—is anything holding the brand back?

For a new launch it is useful to monitor the level and reasons for brand rejection to highlight any immediate issues. This early warning system gives you the opportunity to fix any issues you can, to give the brand the best chance to succeed. Nenycz-Thiel and Romaniuk (2011) outlined some common reasons for rejection:

- *low perceived quality*—often judged by extrinsic qualities such as packaging; having cues that cause possible new buyers to question the brand's performance
- *too expensive*—the price puts off potential buyers, a disincentive to try the brand
- *bad past experience*—product not performing as expected
- *spillover*—particularly for private labels, where negative perceptions of the type of brand in one category, carry over to another category, which may affect variants if they are not distinct from the parent brand.

But don't assume that any lack of repeat buying in a short period of time means that the consumer has rejected the brand. Carefully word any survey questions about brand rejection so category buyers are not led to criticise the brand as a way to rationalise non-buying. Leave room in the possible responses for the fault not being the new launch but rather the marketing, with examples like these:

- a media plan that failed to gain enough reach to build mental availability; or
- a physical availability plan has not made the brand easy to (re)buy.

This stops you from jumping at shadows and fixing exaggerated attitude problems that distract you from more proactive marketing activities.

Conclusion

New brand launches are risky. We have concentrated on trying to reduce that risk by highlighting some areas where it is easy to go astray in thinking and action.

New launches grow by acquiring new customers, who will repeat buy as time progresses. Penetration rules (again); to succeed, you need to recruit your zombie army of many, many category-buyer brains.

The initial customer base of a new launch will skew to heavy category buyers, with larger-than-average repertoires, most of whom become light buyers of the new brand. The statistical reasons for this explain why you should not spend a great deal of money on targeting and recruiting heavy category buyers. These buyers are the easy fish to catch.

For longer-term growth, new launches need to recruit medium and light category buyers. It is therefore dangerous to burst marketing spend at launch, and then have silence for a long period of time. While an initial burst might be needed to help gain physical availability, advertising spend should be spread out as much as possible to avoid wasting money on excess frequency.

To build mental availability, attach the brand to CEPs that are relevant for the wider spectrum of buyers in the category. New launch advertising also needs these characteristics:

- clear category cues to give it context in buyer memory
- excellent branding to build mental availability and to lay the groundwork for building distinctive assets.

Finally, physical availability continues to be vital; advertising (and sales effort) helps to keep as well as build distribution.

11

And Finally, a Bit of Luxury

Byron Sharp and Jenni Romaniuk

An implication is that symbolic brands and even super expensive luxury brands often need to advertise widely. Advertising for luxury watches is not just directed towards billionaires, partly because most people aren't billionaires and because most of the people who buy luxury watches aren't billionaires.

How Brands Grow (2010)

In this chapter we tackle one of the sacred cows of marketing, the luxury brand. We are sceptical of many of the claims for special marketing, and rewriting marketing laws. This chapter is the first of our exploration of the topic.

The growth of wealth

The world is getting richer. In spite of the doom and gloom you may hear in the media, for hundreds of years now the wealth trend has been seriously upwards, and the trend isn't slowing down, quite the opposite. According to Credit Suisse's Global Wealth Report (see Davidson, 2014, for an excellent summary), in 2013 global wealth increased by $21.9 trillion—the largest annual growth since 2000. In one year that's a gain of more than the total loss from the financial crisis in 2007 to 2008, which knocked $21.5 trillion off global wealth.

Contrary to popular belief, it isn't just the rich who are getting richer, far from it; the same forces that propelled *millions* of Europeans and North Americans out of poverty in the twentieth century have been doing the same for *billions* around the world in Asia, Africa and South America. Unsurprisingly, sales of luxury brands are growing. Nowhere is this more evident than in markets like China, India and Russia; today it's rare to hear a luxury brand marketer talking about the future direction of the brand without mentioning these markets.

Maslow's hierarchy of needs suggests that an individual person would have to obtain a fair degree of wealth before they moved from spending on basic needs on to any higher order needs, but this just doesn't appear to be true. Even impoverished people, living on a few dollars a day, spend a non-trivial proportion of their meagre income on things like entertainment—people clearly do not live by bread alone; all of us need a bit of luxury now and then.

Luxury brands are posting impressive growth in developed countries too. Even in everyday necessity categories in wealthy countries, it's common to see a trend towards premium brands. In Kenya households spend about 45% of their household income on food; in France, the proportion is only 14%, because France is a wealthier, more productive, country and this gives people opportunity to spend on more than necessities like food—to buy luxury watches, yachts, and experiences—but the French also, needless to say, eat very well.

Figure 11.1: Projected growth in millionaires in selected countries by 2019

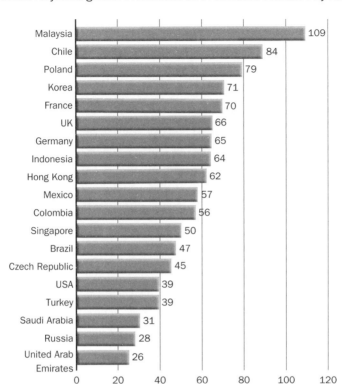

Source: Davidson, 2014

In wealthy countries, few people struggle to buy enough kilojoules; they don't need to buy more food, but they can buy *better, more expensive* food. The (surprisingly belated) arrival of espresso-based coffee and craft beers are just two very obvious signs of this in the USA.

Luxury brands don't just sell to rich people. The super-rich may buy more luxury brands per capita than the rest of us, but it's the middle classes who do most of the buying, because they outnumber the billionaires thousands of times over[1]. This means luxury brands don't sell to everyone but they still compete in mass markets. This statement comes as a surprise,

---

1   Actually, globally there are one million (one thousand thousand) members of the middle class for every single billionaire!

Figure 11.2: Top countries ranked by average wealth

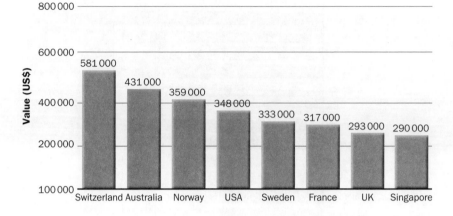

even a rude shock, to many marketers (and marketing theorists) who are openly hostile to the idea. It jars with their belief that the secret to success for any luxury brand is to be seen as exclusive and rare.

The idea is that scarcity sells (or at least maintains high prices) and being seen as popular is supposed to be a kiss of death. In this chapter we explore this theory, because if it is true then luxury brands need different marketing from that advocated in *How Brands Grow*.

Does familiarity breed contempt?

Back in 1995 a French marketing professor and an American marketing consultant attempted to directly study this question. Dubois and Paternault (1995) surveyed 3000 Americans about a list of thirty-four luxury brands[2]. They asked respondents which of the brands they were aware of, which

---

2   The brands were from various product categories: mainly cosmetics, clothing, a few luxury watch brands, one audio equipment brand (Bang & Olufsen), one crystal-ware (Waterford) and one chinaware (Lenox).

they had actually purchased in the past two years, and, finally, they asked respondants to imagine if they had won a contest and could choose a beautiful present, which five brands they would like best. From this survey, for each of the 34 brands, they calculated three metrics:

- awareness
- ownership
- desirability.

Their key thesis was that ownership would reduce desirability, so brands that were owned by many people (high penetration) wouldn't be as desirable.

This is indeed what Dubois and Paternault claimed to find but the research was flawed, which is such a pity because the question was so interesting and important. Mixing categories and brands of vastly different price levels meant that ownership was high for the cosmetic brands like Lancôme and Revlon but desirability less so, while desirability was high for expensive brands like Rolex and Gucci but not ownership. Needless to say people would prefer an expensive luxury watch as a prize than some comparatively cheap lipstick (particularly the men!). Mixing brands of vastly different product categories and different prices guaranteed the authors found what they expected. A flawed study.

Interestingly, the Pierre Cardin brand did rather well on desirability, and not just because of its level of awareness—it scored higher on desirability than some other brands with similar levels of awareness. This result for Pierre Cardin is very interesting and odd—because this brand was the poster child for failing to practise 'exclusivity marketing'. Back in 1995 there would have been many business schools teaching that Pierre Cardin had lost its cachet because it became widely available, and because the brand was no longer just used on haute couture clothing but also perfume, cosmetics, and wine. There is a 2005 *Harvard Business Review* article that says Pierre Cardin overextended itself in the 1990s (Reddy & Terblanche, 2005). Yet oddly the data showed the brand was still desirable to US consumers. Also interestingly, many other haute couture brands have followed Pierre Cardin's lead; for example, today it's very normal for a haute couture house to also sell multiple perfumes under its name.

As often happens, real-world data doesn't nicely fit with (armchair) marketing theory. More research is needed[3], so we looked at awareness, ownership, and desirability of luxury brands across several countries. To avoid the mistakes of the past research we carefully endeavoured to compare brands within the same category and of similar price and quality levels (see Figures 11.3, 11.4, 11.5, 11.6, 11.7 and 11.8). Now would ownership reduce desirability? Would low penetration make a brand more desirable, more exclusive, more cool?

First of all, we found a very tight relationship between awareness and purchase or ownership (a near perfect correlation of around 0.9). Obviously ownership drives awareness (though it isn't guaranteed; what brand is your fridge, your bread-maker, your soap?) and also people are far less likely to buy brands that they haven't heard of—possibly this is especially true for expensive luxury items. Secondly, in each category, awareness is much higher than ownership, which is not unexpected: it shows that awareness cannot be solely due to ownership and that advertising is reaching beyond current customers.

Figure 11.3: Brand awareness and ownership (%) for luxury clothing in Russia, the USA and China (2015)

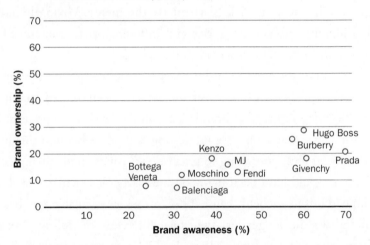

---

3   Actually Paternault and Dubois's study has been replicated but unfortunately with the same flawed design (and analysis). Replication is essential to develop trustworthy scientific knowledge but this is a warning that replicating mistakes does not produce progress. Ideally the first replications should start very close to the original study, as a check against errors and fraud, but subsequent extensions should take different approaches and test different conditions; only then can we learn if a result isn't due purely to the original method or limited conditions (Stern & Ehrenberg, 1997).

Figure 11.4: Brand awareness and ownership (%) for luxury champagne in Russia, the USA and China (2015)

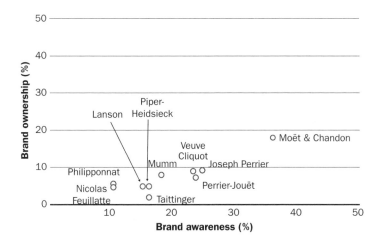

Figure 11.5: Brand awareness and ownership (%) for watches in Russia, the USA and China (2015)

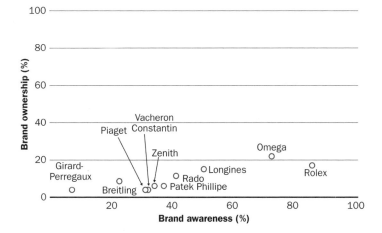

The relationship between awareness and desirability is also strong (correlations of between 0.8 and 0.9). Many luxury brands are not well known, and people don't desire brands they don't know.

Figure 11.6: Brand awareness and desirability (%) for luxury watches in Russia, the USA and China (2015)

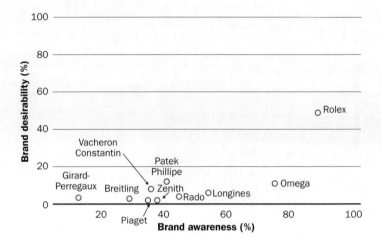

Figure 11.7: Brand awareness and desirability (%) for champagne in Russia, the USA and China (2015)

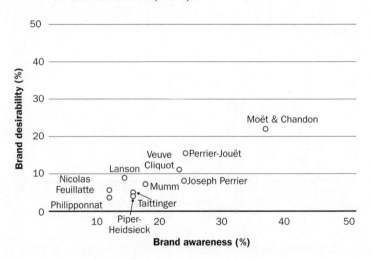

Figure 11.8: Brand awareness and desirability (%) for luxury clothing in Russia, the USA and China (2015)

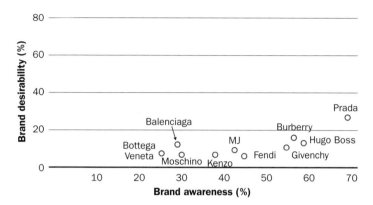

Prada and Rolex are the only slight deviations with extra-high desirability. Both have the highest awareness in their categories (Prada was also presumably helped by the book and movie *The Devil Wears Prada*). But perhaps they are not really deviations at all but rather this is simply a strong double jeopardy effect, where the awareness leaders will also dominate in desirability.

Finally, and directly related to the theory we are testing, the relationship between ownership and desirability is not quite so strong for clothes and watches (correlation of 0.55) where the Prada and Rolex outliers reduce the fit, but the relationship is a very strong for champagne (correlation of 0.9). Presumably the extra high desirability for Prada and Rolex, even given their high awareness, is simply due to their high prices.

The very expensive Patek Phillipe[4] and Vacheron Constantin also deviate—unsurprisingly, their desirability is high their level of ownership and awareness.

---

4   We attempted to include brands that were of similar price and quality to avoid the mistake of the original research by Dubois and Pernault, but didn't quite get it right—these deviations show up the huge flaw in the original research.

These results don't support the familiarity-breeds-contempt theory. They strongly suggest that luxury brands largely compete for mental availability (and presumably physical) just like other brands, and that having more owners (greater penetration) does nothing to depress demand because, even if it did reduce a brand's cachet, exclusivity or coolness, the positive effect of higher mental availability more than compensates.

Figure 11.9: Brand ownership and desirability (%) for luxury clothing in Russia, the USA and China (2015)

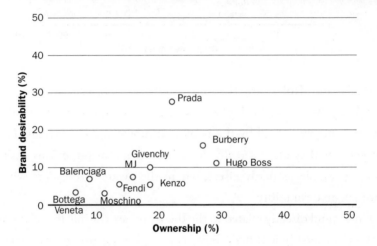

Figure 11.10: Brand ownership and desirability (%) for champagne in Russia, the USA and China (2015)

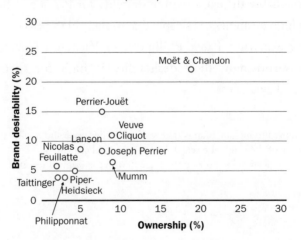

Figure 11.11: Brand ownership and desirability (%) for luxury watches in Russia, the USA and China (2015)

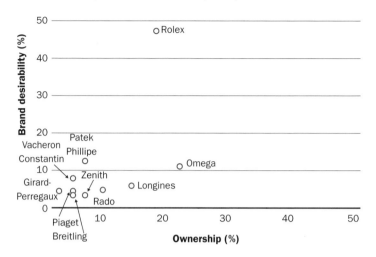

If I own it, does it lose its sparkle?

Finally, to test the proposition that familiarity can breed contempt even further, we looked at individuals', rather than brand level, scores. We looked at people who were aware of a brand and compared the desirability scores of those who owned the brand against those who didn't. Would ownership reduce desirability? Would owners want to collect another, different, luxury brand? If so, how large might this effect be?

But, in spite of some variety seeking which must exist in every market, owning a luxury brand actually results in higher desirability for the brand, even once we have controlled for awareness. Table 11.1 shows the data for luxury clothing brands. We compared two groups of consumers who were aware of the brand: people who owned the brand with people who did not. Desirability was highest amongst owners. Remember that desirability was measured by asking respondents to imagine they had won a competition and could choose a lovely present; they had to select which three brands they would like from each product category. Table 11.1 reports the percentage of owners and non-owners aware of the brand and how many selected the brand as their first choice. We also analysed the results for any choice out of three and the pattern was the same.

Table 11.1 is further evidence that ownership does not decrease desirability. While it is possible that these owners desired the brand even more *before* they bought it, the practical ramifications, if this were true, would be minor; this group still desire the brand more than people who are aware but haven't bought yet.

Table 11.1: Relationship between ownership and desirability for luxury clothing in China, Russia and the USA (2015)

Clothing brand	First-choice desirability (%) amongst owners	First-choice desirability (%) amongst aware non-owners
Prada	43	29
Burberry	23	18
Bottega Veneta	21	8
Hugo Boss	18	11
Givenchy	16	10
Marc Jacobs	14	9
Kenzo	9	7
Balenciaga	9	14
Moschino	8	6
Fendi	8	5
Average	**17**	**12**

Honestly, we expected that there would be a degree of variety seeking large enough to mean that owners would show slightly less desirability than aware non-owners, but the data suggest variety seeking is pretty minor. Instead it seems that loyalty is the natural and dominant behaviour; having bought a brand means you are more likely to buy it again than other consumers who know the brand but haven't bought it (yet).

This effect was weaker for luxury watches, and this fits the idea of variety seeking. Having bought a Rolex, it makes sense that some owners would then prefer another brand as the next to add to their collection. Desirability for Rolex was 51% amongst owners and 51% amongst aware non-owners. Overall the average desirability score across brands was

13.4% for owners and 13.3% for aware non-owners—a much smaller difference than observed for luxury clothes (17% compared with 12%, and champagne: 22% compared with 14%). There is evidence of more variety seeking for luxury watches, but it is still very hard to argue that ownership does much to decrease an individual's desire for that brand.

Does being 'easily available' cheapen a luxury brand?

In another set of data collected in a different survey, this time for a corporate sponsor of the Ehrenberg–Bass Institute, we directly measured perceptions of luxury and exclusivity and we also measured perceptions of physical availability. Would brands with (perceived) restricted distribution be seen as more exclusive, more luxurious?

No, indeed, we found the opposite—brands that were perceived as luxurious and exclusive by more people scored lowest on *not available everywhere* (see Table 11.2). This means perceptions of exclusive distribution do not correlate with a perceptions of exclusivity or luxury. We need to look to other aspects of the marketing mix for the sources of exclusivity (like high price); there is no need to restrict physical availability to make a brand be seen as exclusive or luxurious.

Table 11.2: Perceptions of luxury and relationship with awareness, exclusivity and restricted distribution for alcoholic spirits in the USA (2013)

Luxury brand	Bought in year (%)	Aware (%)	Brand associated with luxury (%)	Brand has a sense of exclusivity (%)	Brand is not available everywhere (%)
Russian vodka	65	91	32	22	8
Mexican tequila	52	80	28	24	13
Scotch whisky 1	46	77	22	19	13
Scotch whisky 2	37	56	19	17	21
European vodka	26	50	15	14	19
US bourbon	21	38	18	15	17
Average	**41**	**65**	**22**	**19**	**15**

Does small mean niched?

These tests of the familiarity-breeds-contempt theory strongly suggest the speculation is wrong: that luxury brands compete like normal brands, within their luxury market. Buying behaviour data that matches the laws set out in *How Brands Grow* supports this.

When we look at how luxury brands compete we see the familiar duplication of purchase law. Brands share customers with all other brands in the category, and more with the larger brands and less with the smaller brands. In Table 11.3 we see that every luxury fashion brand shares about half of its customers with Prada, while they all share far less (about a fifth of their customers) with Bottega Veneta. For those with a deeper interest in the category, a few deviations also worthy of attention appear in the tables: the customer bases of Balenciaga and Bottega Veneta overlap more than expected, perhaps because they are both owned by the same French luxury goods house, Kenzo and Marc Jacobs under-share customer bases, as do Balenciaga and Hugo Boss. The duplication of purchase law clearly highlights these deviations.

The duplication of purchase law also describes well the customer overlap between champagne brands. Once we know the expected pattern, we can see unusually high sharing between Taittinger and Piper Heidsieck. Normally this sort of oversharing occurs between brands with the same owner (and therefore sold through the same distribution network, by the same sales team). That isn't the case here. It may be partly because these two are the smallest brands (note that the two smallest brands of luxury fashion also have high sharing). Buyers of small brands tend to, on average, be heavier category buyers (natural monopoly law), and this may partly explain the high sharing between the two smallest brands in the analysis.

Table 11.5 shows the natural monopoly law in repertoire-size data for luxury watch buyers of each brand. The pattern is clear: owners of smaller brands of luxury watch have larger repertoires. In other words, they are heavier buyers of the category. Remember (from Chapter 2), it's called the natural monopoly law because larger brands tend to *monopolise* the category's light buyers.

Table 11.3: Duplication of purchase table for luxury fashion in China, Russia and the USA (2015)

Customers of	Bought brand (%)	Customers also buying (%)									
		Hugo Boss	Burberry	Prada	Givenchy	Kenzo	Marc J	Fendi	Moschino	Balenciaga	Bottega Veneta
Hugo Boss	31		49	46	42	44	31	27	27	12	15
Burberry	30	52		48	38	31	34	32	28	19	16
Prada	24	59	58		43	42	32	40	29	19	14
Givenchy	21	62	54	50		48	33	37	38	22	20
Kenzo	21	66	44	49	49		25	27	37	16	16
Marc Jacobs	17	57	60	47	42	31		34	29	26	25
Fendi	15	55	61	63	51	37	37		35	25	24
Moschino	13	65	63	55	61	60	38	41		22	23
Balenciaga	10	39	59	49	48	34	46	39	30		39
Bottega Veneta	8	57	57	41	53	41	51	45	37	47	
Average	19	57	56	50	47	41	36	36	32	23	21

Table 11.4: Duplication of purchase table for champagne in China, Russia and the USA (2015)

Customers of	Bought brand (%)	Customers also buying (%)							
		Moët & Chandon	Veuve Clicquot	Joseph Perrier	Perrier-Jouët	Mumm	Lanson	Taittinger	Piper-Heidsieck
Moët & Chandon	20		32	19	24	25	15	20	18
Veuve Clicquot	12	55		22	28	31	20	28	26
Joseph Perrier	10	41	26		34	23	25	30	28
Perrier-Jouët	9	53	36	36		36	20	29	31
Mumm	9	56	40	25	37		19	32	30
Lanson	7	40	32	32	26	23		13	23
Taittinger	7	57	46	39	37	39	13		46
Piper-Heidsieck	7	52	43	39	41	39	25	48	
Average	**10**	**51**	**36**	**30**	**32**	**31**	**20**	**28**	**29**

Table 11.5: Penetration and repertoire size for luxury watches in China, Russia and the USA (2015)

Brand	Owned (%)	Average number of brands ever owned
Omega	67	2.2
Rolex	52	2.1
Longines	45	2.4
Rado	31	2.5
Patek Philippe	19	2.6
Zenith	18	2.8
Breitling	13	2.8
Vacheron Constantin	12	2.7
Piaget	11	2.8
Girard-Perregaux	5	2.9
Average	**27**	**2.6**

If you've only ever bought one luxury watch, then this watch is much more likely to be an Omega or Rolex. But if you own a Girard-Perregaux, then you are probably a bit of a luxury watch collector.

We don't want to overstate the effect; the natural monopoly law is seldom dramatic, but it does show up in market after market, for prosaic items like 'yellow fats' (butter and margarine) and, it seems, for luxury items too.

Finally, unsurprisingly, luxury brands in a category each sell to very similar sorts of buyers. (See Chapter 3 for a discussion on how competing brands typically sell to similar sorts of customers.) For example, luxury clothing brands tend to skew 60:40 or so towards females, all except Hugo Boss, with its bigger men's line, which is the other way round. Champagne brands skew 60:40 towards men. Luxury watches are more 50:50 (except Omega in China, which skews a little to females). Every luxury clothing brand has about half of its buyers aged between 35 and 54 years old, which not surprisingly is a higher proportion than the normal population—young people often lack the funds to buy luxury brands.

Attitudes to luxury brands in general are also similar across brand customer bases. For example, about 30% of buyers *of each brand* of luxury clothing completely agree with the statement, 'luxury brands are a symbol of social status'. Buyer profiles seldom differentiate luxury from one another, nor do those buyers' attitudes to luxury.

Conclusion

In this chapter we explored the widely held beliefs that luxury brands are fundamentally different because high penetration would result in a loss of loyalty, and that they compete for custom in different ways—for example, avoiding mass advertising. These turned out to be myths.

The really obvious difference about luxury brands is that they are very expensive, very high quality and beautiful. Their high quality cannot always be instantly assessed: it may take years of use of a leather bag or a watch to truly appreciate the craftsmanship. Though the quality might be inferred from a high price, there is some danger in using this heuristic and consumers know it. Consequently, it can take a brand many years to build a reputation for extreme quality[5].

Many consumers, particularly those new to a category, don't trust their ability to choose something that is high quality (for example, wine) or fashionable. They look to cues such as price, advertising (how much, how expensive does it look?), and how many other people respect or buy the brand—the fact that they have heard of the brand, or not, consequently

---

5   And it takes decades for a fine wine to prove that it can age and turn into
     something special. Most wines don't. Similarly it takes decades for a luxury brand
     (of watch, car, furniture, jewellery) to prove that retains its value on the secondary
     (e.g. auction) market.

has a powerful effect on the purchasing decision. It's very hard for small, largely unknown brands to sell to these buyers.

All this suggests that luxury brands need a good deal of advertising to build and maintain mental availability. It also suggests that it will take a good deal of time to build the reputation they desire. Ideally, a luxury brand has consistently made beautiful products of exemplary quality for many years. It certainly helps to signal to the market that you have been around for many years: 'Dunhill since 1907', 'Gucci 1921 collection', 'Berry Bros. & Rudd established 1698'.

Finally, it's important to remember that despite what can seem like outrageous prices, luxury brands get most of their sales from the middle class, not a small cadre of billionaires. More bottles of Château Lafite Rothschild and Penfold's Grange are sold to doctors and lawyers than business magnates[6]. Indeed many bottles of fine wine are bought by currently impoverished medical and law students, saving or pooling their money to try something special now and then (for example, on a special occasion, such as graduation). The Brookings Institution estimates that there were 1.8 billion people in the global middle class in 2009 and that this number is rising so rapidly that the global middle class will reach 3.2 billion by the end of 2020 (Yueh, 2013). In comparison, there are only 1600 or so billionaires on the planet, far too small a market to sustain most luxury brands.

---

6   The few billionaires on the planet can only drink so much wine. Indeed some drink none: for example, neither Donald Trump nor Warren Buffet drink any type of alcohol drink—though this has not deterred Trump from marketing Trump Vodka nor Buffet from making investments in alcohol distribution companies.

A Final Note

Thank you for reading *How Brands Grow, Part 2*. We hope it will help you and your colleagues make evidence-based marketing decisions.

Our hope is that these laws become commonplace in brand strategy discussions—that marketers, for example, query how a tactic might help move the brand up the double jeopardy line, draw on the duplication of purchase law to identify opportunities in a category, and quantify the strength of their distinctive assets so they can be built and protected accordingly. For marketing to be taken seriously in the boardroom, it needs this rigour.

We also hope that the ubiquity of these laws makes you think twice when a new technology or media claims to be revolutionising how to undertake marketing. We might have different tactics to influence category buyers but that doesn't change the fundamental need for building mental and physical availability, which means that *reach is not optional*.

We have really tried to push the boundaries of many laws, with testing in markets as diverse as Turkey and Nigeria, and categories ranging from banking, mobile phones, social media, coronary stents and that sacred cow, luxury brands. People may say their market is different, and it might be (a bit), but rarely does any difference rewrite the laws of growth. Don't take our word for it: do test these laws in your own categories.

There is much more work to be done. As you read this, teams of Ehrenberg–Bass Institute researchers are building further knowledge in areas such as portfolio management, category growth, brand health measurement, advertising and media strategy, and shopper behaviour. It is exciting to be entering into the age of marketing enlightenment.

Our work continues. If you would like to be part of this, please do not hesitate to be in touch.

Jenni and Byron

www.MarketingScience.info

Reference List

Allsopp, J, Sharp B & Dawes J 2004, 'The double jeopardy line—empirical results', Australia and New Zealand Marketing Academy (ANZMAC) conference, 29 November, Victoria University, Wellington, New Zealand.

Anderson, JR & Bower, GH 1979, *Human Associative Memory*, Lawrence Erlbaum, Hillsdale, NJ.

Anesbury, Z, Nenycz-Thiel, M, Kennedy, R & Dawes, J 2014, 'Shopping takes only seconds ... in-store and online', Report 65, Ehrenberg–Bass Institute for Marketing Science, Adelaide.

Anschuetz, N 2002, 'Why a brand's most valuable consumer is the next one it adds', *Journal Of Advertising Research*, vol. 42, no. 1, pp. 15–21.

Atsmon, Y & Magni, M 2012, 'Meet the Chinese consumer of 2020', *McKinsey & Company: Insights and Publications*, March, <www.mckinsey.com/insights/asia-pacific/meet_the_chinese_consumer_of_2020>, accessed 10 July 2015.

Bain & Co. 2013, 'Customer loyalty in retail banking: Global edition', *Bain & Company*, <www.bain.com/publications/articles/customer-loyalty-in-retail-banking-2013.aspx>, accessed 11 July 2015.

Baldinger, AL, Blair, E & Echambadi, R 2002, 'Why brands grow', *Journal of Advertising Research*, vol. 1, pp. 7–14.

Bass, FM & King, CW 1968, 'The theory of first purchase of new products', Purdue University, Institute for Research in the Behavioral, Economic, and Management Sciences.

Bayne, T, Samuels, B & Sharp, B 2014, 'Marketing banks: target new, not loyal customers', *Admap*, April, pp. 40–1, available from *Warc*, <www.warc.com>.

Bell, DR 2014, *Location is (Still) Everything: The Surprising Influence of the Real World on How We Search, Shop and Sell in the Virtual One*, Amazon Publishing.

Bennett, D 2008, 'Brand loyalty dynamics—China's television brands come of age', *Australasian Marketing Journal*, vol. 16, no. 2, pp. 39–50.

Binet, L & Field, P 2009, 'Empirical generalisations about advertising campaign success', *Journal of Advertising Research*, vol. 49, no. 2, pp. 130–3.

Bird, M & Channon, C 1969, 'Brand usage, brand image, and advertising policy—part I', *Admap*, vol. 6, pp. 27–46.

Bird, M, Channon, C & Ehrenberg, ASC 1970, 'Brand image and brand usage', *Journal of Marketing Research*, vol. 7, no. 3, pp. 307–14.

Bogomolova, S & Romaniuk, J 2009, 'Brand defection in a business-to-business financial service', *Journal of Business Research*, vol. 62, no. 3, pp. 291–6.

Ceber, M 2009, 'The importance of light TV viewers and how to reach them', Master's thesis, University of South Australia, Adelaide.

Cohen, J, Lockshin, L & Sharp, B 2012, 'A better understanding of the structure of a wine market using the attribute of variety', *International Journal of Business and Globalisation*, vol. 8, no. 1, pp. 66–80.

Davidson, L 2014, 'Credit Suisse Global Wealth Report: are you among the world's richest?', *The Telegraph*, 14 October.

Dawes, J 2013, 'Reasons for variation in SCR for private label brands', *European Journal of Marketing*, vol. 47, no. 11/12, pp. 1804–24.

Dawes, J & Nenycz-Thiel, M 2014, 'Comparing retailer purchase patterns and brand metrics for in-store and online grocery purchasing', *Journal of Marketing Management*, vol. 30, no. 3–4, pp. 364–82.

Dubois, B & Paternault, C 1995, 'Understanding the world of international luxury brands: the "dream formula"', *Journal of Advertising Research*, July/August, pp. 69–76.

East, R & Hammond, K 2006, 'Multi-category research on the impact of positive and negative word of mouth on brand choice', European Marketing Academy Conference (EMAC), 23–26 May, Athens Business and Economics University, Athens, Greece

East, R, Hammond, K & Lomax, W 2008, 'Measuring the impact of positive and negative word of mouth on brand purchase probability', *International Journal of Research in Marketing*, vol. 25, no. 3, pp. 215–24.

East, R, Hammond, K & Wright, M 2007, 'The relative incidence of positive and negative word of mouth: a multi-category study', *International Journal of Research in Marketing*, vol. 24, no. 2, pp. 175–84.

East, R., Romaniuk, J & Lomax, W 2011, 'The NPS and the ACSI: a critique and an alternative metric', *International Journal of Market Research*, vol. 53, no. 3, p. 15.

East, R., Uncles, M, Romaniuk, J & Dall'Olmo, R 2015, 'Antecedents to word of mouth', *International Journal of Market Research* forthcoming.

Economic Times 2015, 'Vodafone launches special plans for iPhone 6, 6+, other models', *Economic Times*, 16 January.

The Economist 2014, 'Chinese consumers: doing it their way', *The Economist*.

Ehrenberg, A 1972, *Repeat Buying: Theory and Applications*, American Elsevier, New York.

Ehrenberg, A 2000, 'Repeat-buying: facts, theory and applications', *Journal of Empirical Generalisations in Marketing Science*, vol. 5, pp. 392–770.

Ehrenberg, ASC 1959, 'The pattern of consumer purchases', *Applied Statistics*, vol. 8, no. 1, pp. 26–41.

Ehrenberg, ASC & Goodhardt, G 2001, 'New brands: near-instant loyalty' *Journal of Targeting, Measurement and Analysis for Marketing*, vol. 10, no. 1, pp. 9–17.

Ehrenberg, ASC, Goodhardt, G & Barwise, TP 1990, 'Double jeopardy revisited', *Journal of Marketing*, vol. 54, no. 3, pp. 82–91.

Epstein, E, 2014, 'The Johnnie Walker brand: a rich blend of design and progress', *Mashable*, 3 May, <http://mashable.com/2014/05/02/johnnie-walker-marketing-strategy/>, accessed 26 June 2015.

Fader, PS & Schmittlein, DC 1993, 'Excess behavioral loyalty for high-share brands: deviations from the Dirichlet model for repeat purchasing', *Journal of Marketing Research*, vol. 30, no. 4, pp. 478–93.

Faulkner, M, Truong, O & Romaniuk, J 2014, 'Uncovering generalized patterns of brand competition in China', *Journal of Product & Brand Management*, vol. 23, no. 7, pp. 554–71.

Gaillard, E, Sharp, A & Romaniuk, J 2006, 'Measuring brand distinctive elements in an in-store packaged goods consumer context', European Marketing Academy Conference (EMAC), 23–26 May, Athens Business and Economics University, Athens, Greece.

Goodhardt, GJ & Ehrenberg, ASC 1969, 'Duplication of television viewing between and within channels', *Journal of Marketing Research*, vol. 6, May, pp. 169–78.

Goodhardt, GJ, Ehrenberg, ASC & Chatfield, C 1984, 'The Dirichlet: comprehensive model of buying behaviour', *Journal of the Royal Statistical Society*, vol. 147, no. 5, pp. 621–55.

Greenfield, S 2000, *The Private Life of the Brain*, Allen Lane, London.

Hammond, K, Ehrenberg, ASC & Goodhardt, GJ 1996, 'Market segmentation for competitive brands', *European Journal of Marketing*, vol. 30, no. 12, pp. 39–49.

Harrison, F 2013, 'Digging deeper down into the empirical generalization of brand recall', *Journal of Advertising Research*, vol. 53, no. 1, pp. 181–5.

Hartnett, N 2011, 'Distinctive assets and advertising effectiveness', Master's thesis, University of South Australia, Adelaide.

Holden, SJ & Lutz, RJ 1992, 'Ask not what the brand can evoke; ask what can evoke the brand?', *Advances in Consumer Research*, vol. 19, no. 1, pp. 101–7.

Howard, JA & Sheth, JN 1969, *The Theory of Buyer Behavior*, John & Wiley Sons, New York.

Huffington Post 2013, 'The U.S. illiteracy rate hasn't changed in 10 years', *Huffington Post*, 6 September.

Joseph, S 2015, 'Unilever CMO Keith Weed lifts lid on plan to push marketing beyond brand development', *The Drum*, 2 June.

Kearns, Z, Millar, S & Lewis, T 2000, 'Dirichlet deviations and brand growth', Australia and New Zealand Marketing Academy (ANZMAC) conference, 28 November – 1 December, Griffith University, Gold Coast, Queensland.

Kennedy, R & Ehrenberg, A 2001, 'Competing retailers generally have the same sorts of shoppers', *Journal of Marketing Communications*, vol. 7, no. 1, pp. 19–26.

Kennedy, R, Ehrenberg, A & Long, S 2000, 'Competitive brands' user-profiles hardly differ', Market Research Society Conference (UK), 15–17 March, Brighton, UK.

KPMG 2014, 'E-commerce in China: driving a new consumer culture', *China 360*, no. 15.

Livaditis, M, Sharp, A & Sharp, B 2012, 'Evidence of naturally bias behaviour—seating habits at a lecture', Australia and New Zealand Marketing Academy (ANZMAC) conference, 3–5 December, Ehrenberg–Bass Institute for Marketing Science, Adelaide.

Lockshin, L & Cohen, E 2011, 'Using product and retail choice attributes for cross-national segmentation', *European Journal of Marketing*, vol. 45, no. 7/8, pp. 1236–52.

McCabe, J, Stern, P & Dacko, SG 2013, 'Purposeful empiricism: how stochastic modeling informs industrial marketing research', *Industrial Marketing Management*, vol. 42, no. 3, pp. 421–32.

Mccormick, A 2011, 'Are virtual walls the future of retail?', *Wallblog*, 20 September, <http://wallblog.co.uk/2011/09/20/are-virtual-walls-the-future-of-retail/>, accessed 2 July 2015.

McDonald, C & Ehrenberg, ASC 2003, 'What happens when brands gain or lose share?: customer acquisition or increased loyalty?', Report 31 for corporate members, Ehrenberg–Bass Institute for Marketing Science, Adelaide.

McPhee, WN 1963, *Formal Theories of Mass Behaviour*, The Free Press of Glencoe, New York.

Major, J 2014, 'Drawing the spotlight? Investigating the attention grabbing potential of distinctive assets', Master's thesis, University of South Australia, Adelaide.

Major, J, Tanaka, A & Romaniuk, J 2014, 'The competitive battleground of colours, logos and taglines in brand identity', in G. Muratovski (ed.), *Design For Business*, pp. 42–59, Intellect Ltd, Bristol, UK.

Mangold, WG, Miller, F & Brockway, GR 1999, 'Word-of-mouth communication in the service marketplace', *Journal of Services Marketing*, vol. 13, no. 1, pp. 73–89.

Martin, C, Jr 1973, 'The theory of double jeopardy', *Journal of the Academy of Marketing Science*, vol. 1, no. 2, pp. 148–56.

Meeker, M, & Wu, L 2013, 'Internet trends, D11 conference', *KPCB*, <www.slideshare.net/kleinerperkins/kpcb-internet-trends-2013>, accessed 25 June 2015.

Melis, K, Campo, K, Breugelmans, E & Lamey, L 2015, 'The impact of the multi-channel retail mix on online store choice: does online experience matter?', *Journal of Retailing*, in press.

Moth, 2015, 'UK online retail sales to reach £52.25bn in 2015: report', <https://econsultancy.com/blog/66007-uk-online-retail-sales-to-reach-52-25bn-in-2015-report>, *Econsultancy*, accessed 26 January 2015.

Mundt, K, Dawes, J & Sharp, B 2006, 'Can a brand outperform competitors on cross-category loyalty? An examination of cross-selling metrics in two financial services markets', *Journal of Consumer Marketing*, vol. 23, no. 7, pp. 465–9.

Nelson-Field, K, Riebe, E & Sharp, B 2012, 'What's not to "like"?: can a Facebook fan base give a brand the advertising reach it needs?' *Journal of Advertising Research*, vol. 52, no. 2, pp. 262–9.

Nenycz-Thiel, M & Romaniuk, J 2011, 'The nature and incidence of private label rejection', *Australasian Marketing Journal*, vol. 19, pp. 93–9.

Newstead, K, Taylor, J, Kennedy, R & Sharp, B 2009, 'The long-term sales effects of advertising: lessons from single source,' *Journal of Advertising Research*, vol. 49, no. 2, pp. 207–10.

Nielsen 2014, 'Nielsen: China sees more sophisticated online shoppers', <www.nielsen.com/content/dam/nielsenglobal/cn/docs/Nielsen%202014%20 China%20online%20shopper%20trends_EN_Client%20Version.PDF>, accessed 10 July 2015.

Nielsen 2015, 'The future of grocery: e-commerce, digital technology and changing shopping preferences around the world', <www.nielsen.com/ content/dam/nielsenglobal/vn/docs/Reports/2015/Nielsen%20Global%20 E-Commerce%20and%20The%20New%20Retail%20Report%20 APRIL%202015%20%28Digital%29.pdf>, Nielsen, accessed 10 July 2015.

Ovington, L, McIntyre, E, Saliba, A & Bruwer, J 2014, 'Why do people avoid wine? Comparisons across Australia, Canada, United Kingdom, United States and India', *Wine and Viticulture Journal*, vol. 29, no. 4, pp. 63–5.

Pare, V & Dawes, J 2011, 'The persistence of excess brand loyalty over multiple years', *Marketing Letters*, vol. 21, no. 2, pp. 163–75.

Pickford, C & Goodhardt, G 2000, 'An empirical study of buying behaviour in an industrial market', Academy of Marketing Annual Conference (AM2000), 5–7 July, University of Derby, Derby, UK.

Press Trust of India 2013, 'Samsung beats Nokia to top spot in Inida, Apple posts strong gains: survey', *NDTV Gadgets*, 21 August, <http://gadgets.ndtv.com/ mobiles/news/samsung-beats-nokia-to-top-spot-in-india-apple-posts-strong-gains-survey-408478>, accessed 24 June 2015.

Reddy, M & Terblanche, N 2005, 'How not to extend your luxury brand', *Harvard Business Review*, December, <https://hbr.org/2005/12/how-not-to-extend-your-luxury-brand>, accessed 2 July 2015.

Redford, N. 2005, 'Regularities in media consumption', Master's thesis, University of South Australia, Adelaide.

Reichheld, FF 2003, 'The one number you need to grow', *Harvard Business Review*, December, pp. 46–54.

Riebe, E, Wright, M, Stern, P & Sharp, B 2014, 'How to grow a brand: retain or acquire customers?', *Journal of Business Research*, vol. 67, no. 5, pp. 990–7.

Roberts, K 2004, *Lovemarks: The Future Beyond Brands*, Murdoch Books, Sydney.

Romaniuk, J 2003, 'Brand attributes—"distribution outlets" in the mind', *Journal of Marketing Communications*, vol. 9, June, pp. 73–92.

Romaniuk, J 2008, 'Comparing methods of measuring brand personality traits', *Journal of Marketing Theory and Practice*, vol. 16, no. 2, pp. 153–61.

Romaniuk, J 2009, 'The efficacy of brand-execution tactics in TV advertising, brand placements and internet advertising', *Journal of Advertising Research*, vol. 49, no. 2, pp. 143–50.

Romaniuk, J 2013, 'Modeling mental market share', *Journal of Business Research*, vol. 66, no. 2, pp. 188–95.

Romaniuk, J, Beal, V & Uncles, M 2013, 'Achieving reach in a multi-media environment: how a marketer's first step provides the direction for the second', *Journal of Advertising Research*, vol. 53, no. 2, pp. 221–30.

Romaniuk, J, Bogomolova, S & Dall'Olmo Riley, F 2012, 'Brand image and brand usage: is a forty-year-old empirical generalization still useful?', *Journal of Advertising Research*, vol. 52, no. 2, pp. 243–51.

Romaniuk, J & Dawes, J 2005, 'Loyalty to price tiers in purchases of bottled wine', *Journal of Product and Brand Management*, vol. 14, no. 1, pp. 57–64.

Romaniuk, J, Dawes, J & Nenycz-Thiel, M 2014a, 'Generalizations regarding the growth and decline of manufacturer and store brands', *Journal of Retailing and Consumer Services*, vol. 21, no. 5, pp. 725–34.

Romaniuk, J., Dawes & Nenycz-Thiel, M 2014b, 'Understanding patterns of brand share growth and decline in emerging markets', European Marketing Academy Conference (EMAC), 3–6 June, University of Valencia, Valencia, Spain.

Romaniuk, J & Gaillard, E 2007, 'The relationship between unique brand associations, brand usage and brand performance: analysis across eight categories', *Journal of Marketing Management*, vol. 23, no. 3, pp. 267–84.

Romaniuk, J & Hartnett, N 2010, 'Understanding, identifying and building distinctive brand assets', Report 52, Ehrenberg–Bass Institute for Marketing Science, Adelaide.

Romaniuk J, & Nenycz-Thiel M 2014, 'Measuring the strength of color–brand name links', *Journal of Advertising Research*, vol. 54, no. 3, pp. 313–19.

Romaniuk, J, Nenycz-Thiel, M & Truong, O 2011, 'Do consumers reject brands? Which, where and how often', Report 61, Ehrenberg–Bass Institute for Marketing Science, Adelaide.

Romaniuk, J & Nicholls, E 2006, 'Evaluating advertising effects on brand perceptions: incorporating prior knowledge', *International Journal of Market Research*, vol. 48, no. 2, pp. 179–92.

Romaniuk, J & Sharp, B 2000, 'Using known patterns in image data to determine brand positioning', *International Journal of Market Research*, vol. 42, no. 2, pp. 219–30.

Romaniuk, J & Sharp, B 2003, '"Pareto share" in customer knowledge based brand knowledge', Australia and New Zealand Marketing Academy (ANZMAC) conference, 3–5 December, Ehrenberg–Bass Institute for Marketing Science, Adelaide.

Romaniuk, J & Sharp, B 2004, 'Conceptualizing and measuring brand salience', *Marketing Theory*, vol. 4, no. 4, pp. 327–42.

Romaniuk, J & Wight, S 2009, 'The influence of brand usage on responses to advertising awareness measures', *International Journal of Market Research*, vol. 51, no. 2, pp. 203–18.

Romaniuk, J & Wight, S 2014, 'The stability and sales contribution of heavy buying households', *Journal of Consumer Behaviour*, vol. 14, no. 1, pp. 13–20.

Rosch, E & Mervis, CB 1975, 'Family resemblances: studies in the internal structure of categories', *Cognitive Psychology*, vol. 7, pp. 573–605.

Rubinson, J 2009, 'Empirical evidence of TV advertising effectiveness', *Journal of Advertising Research*, vol. 49, no. 2, pp. 220–6.

Safi 2015, 'About us', *Safi*, <http://safi.com.my/web-en/about-us/safi-philosophy. php>, accessed 25 June 2015.

Sawyer, A, Noel, H & Janiszewski, C 2009, 'The spacing effects of multiple exposures on memory: implications for advertising scheduling', *Journal of Advertising Research*, vol. 49, no. 2, pp. 193–7.

Scriven, J & Ehrenberg, ASC 2003, 'How consumers choose prices over time', Report 32 for corporate members, Ehrenberg–Bass Institute for Marketing Science, Adelaide.

Sharp, B 2009, 'Detroit's real problem: it's customer acquisition, not loyalty', *Marketing Research*, Spring, pp. 26–7.

Sharp, B 2013, *Marketing: Theory, Evidence, Practice*, Oxford University Press, Melbourne.

Sharp, B, Beal, V & Collins, M 2009, 'Television: back to the future', *Journal of Advertising Research*, vol. 49, no. 2, pp. 211–29.

Sharp, B, Newstead, K, Beal, V, Tanusondjaja, A & Kennedy, R 2014, 'Key media principles', Report 66, Ehrenberg–Bass Institute for Marketing Science, Adelaide.

Sharp, B & Romaniuk, J 2007, 'There is a Pareto law—but not as you know it', Report 42 for corporate sponsors, Ehrenberg–Bass Institute for Marketing Science, Adelaide.

Sharp, B, Trinh, G & Dawes, J 2014, 'What makes heavy buyers so heavy? Do they favour you or just eat a lot?' Report 65, Ehrenberg–Bass Institute for Marketing Science, Adelaide.

Sharp, B, Wright, M & Goodhardt, G 2002, 'Purchase loyalty is polarised into either repertoire or subscription patterns,' *Australasian Marketing Journal*, vol. 10, no. 3, pp. 7–20.

Singh, J, Scriven, J, Clemente, M, Lomax, W & Wright, M 2012, 'New brand extensions: patterns of success and failure', *Journal of Advertising Research*, vol. 52, no. 2, pp. 234–42.

Smith, R 2011, 'In tribute to Wells, banks try the hard sell', *Wall Street Journal*, 28 February, <www.wsj.com/articles/SB10001424052748704430304576170702480420980>, accessed 9 July 2015.

Statista 2015, 'Number of digital shoppers in the United States from 2010 to 2018 (in millions)', Statista: The Statistics Portal, <ww.statista.com/statistics/183755/number-of-us-internet-shoppers-since-2009/>, accessed 4 July 2015.

Stern, P & Ehrenberg, A 1997, 'Replication means extension', European Marketing Academy Conference (EMAC), 20–23 May University of Warwick, Conventry, UK.

Sugawara, T 2014, 'Alibaba taps countryside for 600 million more customers', *Nikkei Asian Review*, 6 December, <http://asia.nikkei.com/Business/Companies/Alibaba-taps-countryside-for-600-million-more-customers>, accessed 2 July 2015.

Sylvester, AK, McQueen, J & Moore, SD 1994, 'Brand growth and "phase 4" marketing', *Admap*, September, available from *Warc*, <www.warc.com>.

Tang, Y, Zhang, W, Chen, K, Feng, S, Ji, Y, Shen, J, Reiman, E & Lui, Y 2006, 'Arithmetic processing in the brain shaped by cultures', *Proceedings of the National Academy of Sciences*, vol. 103, July, pp. 10775–80.

Taylor, JW 1977, 'A Striking Characteristic of Innovators', *Journal of Marketing Research*, vol. 14, February, pp. 104–7.

Taylor, J, Kennedy, R & Sharp, B 2009, 'Making generalizations about advertising's convex sales response function: is once really enough?', *Journal of Advertising Research*, vol. 49, no. 2, pp. 198–200.

Trinh, GT, Romaniuk, J & Tanusondjaja, A 2015, 'Benchmarking buyer behavior towards new brands', *Marketing Letters*, DOI 10.1007/s11002-015-9376-8.

Troung, O 2014, 'Do consumer behaviour empirical generalisations hold in emerging markets?', Master's thesis, University of South Australia.

Truong, O, Faulkner, M & Mueller Loose, S 2012, 'An examination of consumer profiles across brands in emerging markets', Australia and New Zealand Marketing Academy (ANZMAC) conference, 3–5 December, Ehrenberg–Bass Institute for Marketing Science, Adelaide.

Truong, O, Romaniuk, J & Nenycz-Thiel, M 2011, 'The incidence of brand rejection in FMCG categories', Australia and New Zealand Marketing Academy (ANZMAC) conference, 28–30 November, Edith Cowan University, Perth.

Tulving, E & Craik, FIM 2000, *The Oxford Handbook of Memory*, Oxford University Press, Oxford.

Uncles, M, East, R & Lomax, W 2010, 'Market share is correlated with word-of-mouth volume', *Australasian Marketing Journal*, vol. 18, pp. 145–50.

Uncles, M & Hammond, K 1995, 'Grocery store patronage', *International Review of Retail, Distribution & Consumer Research*, vol. 5, no. 3, pp. 287–302.

Uncles, M, Kennedy, R, Nenycz-Thiel, M, Singh, J & Kwok, S 2012, 'User profiles for directly competing brands seldom differ: reexamining the evidence', *Journal of Advertising Research*, vol. 52, no. 2, pp. 252–61.

Uncles, MD 2010, 'Retail change in China: retrospect and prospect', *International Review of Retail, Distribution and Consumer Research*, vol. 20, no. 1, pp. 69–84.

Uncles, MD & Ehrenberg, A 1990, 'The buying of packaged goods at US retail chains', *Journal of Retailing*, vol. 66, no. 3, pp. 278–96.

Uncles, MD, Hammond, KA, Ehrenberg, ASC & Davies, RE 1994, 'A replication study of two brand-loyalty measures', *European Journal of Operational Research*, vol. 76, no. 2, pp. 375–85.

Uncles, MD & Kwok, S 2008, 'Generalizing patterns of store-type patronage: an analysis across major Chinese cities', *International Review of Retail, Distribution and Consumer Research*, vol. 18, no. 5, pp. 473–93.

Uncles, MD & Kwok, S 2009, 'Patterns of store patronage in urban China', *Journal of Business Research*, vol. 62, no. 1, pp. 68–81.

Watts, DJ & Dodds, PS 2007, 'Influentials, networks, and public opinion formation', *Journal of Consumer Research*, vol. 34, no. 4, pp. 441–58.

Wentz, L 2013, 'A leader in Latin-influenced food market, Goya enters baby aisle', *Advertising Age*, <http://adage.com/article/hispanic-marketing/a-leader-changing-market-goya-enters-baby-food-aisle/243089/>, accessed 9 July 2015.

Wilbur, K & Farris, P 2013, 'Distribution and market share', *Journal of Retailing*, vol. 90, no. 2, pp. 154–67.

Winchester, M & Romaniuk, J 2008, 'Negative brand beliefs and brand usage', *International Journal of Market Research*, vol. 50, no. 3, pp. 355–75.

Winchester, M, Romaniuk, J & Bogomolova, S 2008, 'Positive and negative brand beliefs and brand defection/uptake', *European Journal of Marketing*, vol. 42, no. 5/6, pp. 553–70.

Wragg, C & Regan, T 2012, 'Marketing food: Quorn's new appeal', *Admap*, November, pp. 32–3, available from *Warc*, <www.warc.com>

Wright, M & Sharp, A 2001, 'The effect of a new brand entrant on a market', *Journal of Empirical Generalisations in Marketing Science*, vol. 6, pp. 15–29.

Yueh, L 2013, 'The rise of the global middle class', *BBC News*, 19 June.